THE TECHNIQUES OF
CROCHETED & OPENWORK LACE

THE TECHNIQUES OF
CROCHETED & OPENWORK LACE

ENA MAIDENS

B.T. Batsford Ltd.,Ltd. London

Acknowledgements

I wish to take this opportunity to thank all my friends and helpers who have encouraged me to set down what experience over the years has taught me. I am especially grateful to those who have coped with my instructions, particularly my good friend Vera Humphrey, who agreed to all my requests with unfailing good humour.

My thanks and appreciation I would like to give to Ken Hoskins AIIP, ARPS, AMPA (Kitchenham's Ltd) of Bournemouth, whose photographs gave me much confidence and to Bev Johnston, whose line drawings were a splendid understanding of a quite difficult subject.

I would also like to express my gratitude to my typists: Olive Hall for adapting to unfamiliar territory, and Gail Taylor for not only bringing me her typing but also her enthusiasm.

I give my admiration and thanks to my husband for his ability to cope under all circumstances, and I am grateful to Mrs Jean Dudding for allowing me to include her tray design of Coggeshall lace *(figure 53)* and Mrs Riley for a charming table mat *(figure 54)*. The collar in figure 45 was kindly loaned by Mrs Dyke, figure 46 is reproduced by courtesy of Mrs Betty Pond, and figures 48–52 by courtesy of Scaplan's Court Museum, Poole, Dorset.

First published 1982
© Ena Maidens 1982

ISBN 0 7134 2568 7

Filmset in Monophoto Plantin by
Servis Filmsetting Ltd, Manchester

Printed in Great Britain by
The Anchor Press Ltd, Tiptree, Essex
for the publishers,
B.T. Batsford Ltd,
4 Fitzhardinge Street, London, W1H 0AH

CONTENTS

Introduction: crocheted and openwork lace, its affiliation to other crafts

This technique covers such a wide field, and it is fascinating to uncover the many other crafts which have influenced its present day appearance. Crochet, like knitting, is believed to trace its roots back to the days of ancient Egypt, although its exact origin is not proved.

Tambour embroidery was certainly worked 2000 to 3000 years before Christ, first of all in China. This was worked on material stretched across a drum-shaped frame, the thread being pulled through the material to the surface by a fine hook. This Tambour embroidery travelled on through many countries in Asia, borrowing a little from each country, until it halted for a while in Turkey. Here it still decorated garments, but these were mainly for the women in harems. The work was richly decorative, but unfortunately never seen outside the apartments of the women.

Eventually, in the sixteenth century, there began another revival, and in convents nuns worked lace to the early written instructions. Unfortunately the majority of the patterns have been destroyed owing, it is said, to the style which was used at that time to outline or prick the patterns. It is therefore difficult to follow the evolution of the crafts, but it has been recorded that the monks demanded a very high standard for the beautifying of the Church. Nevertheless, it would have been of great interest to see at what stage it was decided to dispense with the material background and connect the loops with chains.

For many centuries crochet continued to copy the exquisite designs of Venetian point, but it was not until the famine years of 1840 that the refugees fleeing from France introduced crochet to Ireland as a cottage industry, the word 'Crochet' meaning a hook. The standard of work produced became very high and many centres became famous, Clones, in the North, being noted for very fine work. Irish crochet became very much admired in Victorian times in Britain but unfortunately the work became inferior in quality, owing to the great demand for it, and the industry began to fail.

During the two wars which followed in the twentieth century crochet was at a low ebb and it was not until the middle 'fifties that interest began to revive. The advent of new textile techniques coincided with a demand from the younger generation for a re-volutionary change in fashion, and the fashion designers seized the opportunity to use something different, namely knitting and crochet.

The appeal of crochet has always been its quickness in obtaining a result and the durability in its wear. It is also helped by the fact that in place of long, written instructions there has come abbreviated notation. Its advantage is that, as in tapestry or cross stitch, the design can be seen at once, and this encourages the worker. On the Continent, in Germany and France, working symbols are practically identical in each country and very adventurous, while in Britain they are very little different and have caught up. Japan, however, is using a different set of symbols, but the advantage of them all is that no words are really necessary, and this can only be good for stimulating new ideas.

Conversion chart for crochet hooks

UK	USA	EUROPE
7 mm	K/10½	7
6.5 mm	J/10	6.5
6 mm	I/9	6
5.5 mm	H/8	5
5 mm		5
4.5 mm	G/6	4.5
4 mm	F/5	4
3.5 mm	E/4	3.5
3 mm	C/2	3
2.5 mm	B/1	2.5

Abbreviations

UK		USA	
st	stitch		
cl	cluster		
blks	blocks		
sp	space		
gr	group		
y o h	yarn over hook	y o	yarn over
inc	increase		
dec	decrease		
p	picot		

Chart for crochet terms

UK		USA	
ch	chain	ch	chain
dc	double crochet	sc	single crochet
tr	treble	dc	double crochet
h tr	half treble	h dc	half double crochet
dbl tr	double treble		
trip tr	triple treble	tr	treble
quad tr	quadruple treble	dbl tr	double treble
		trip tr	triple treble
quin tr	quintuple treble	quad tr	quadruple treble
ss	slip stitch	ss	slip stitch

1 BASIC CROCHET

Tools and materials

The choice of materials in the twentieth century is vast and caters for all tastes and age groups.

Wool and cotton are always firm favourites and pure silk and tussore have reappeared after a long absence. The Yorkshire mills spin an amazing quality of soft wools from 2 ply to chunky ply and they are always willing to send sample cards for quality and colours. Mohair is always popular and much favoured by the younger generation. The greater number of yarns at this time are mixed with synthetic fibres, thus making for ease in washing and wear. Shetland wool is always in demand and ranges from 1 ply to double knitting. Welsh wool obtained from the local sheep is perhaps one of the hardest wearing, with good colours. Scottish wool is world famous not only for its softness but for the gentle shades of colour taken from the heather and misty hills. Scandinavia is noted for its particular yarns such as Lopi, used mainly for its sweaters in mute shades. Germany and France have a variety of lurex yarns and fine mohairs.

The list and variety is endless in both the UK and USA, with such names as Bernat Klein, Columbia Minerva, Bucilla, Reynolds and many other well known yarns. Cottons are always of a consistent quality, supplied by Coats of Scotland in the UK and DMC in Europe. The USA have J.P. Coats and Clarke and the American Thread Co., to name two.

To work this array of materials there is a choice of methods for all talents, depending upon how one wishes to experiment. Figure 1 shows crochet hooks of steel and metal, a Tunisian crochet hook, a broomstick pin, a small size hairpin, a gauge and tambour hooks. In the following pages it will be shown what use these tools can be put to.

However, it must be understood that in buying

Fig. 1 *At the back, from left to right:* a broomstick pin, a Tunisian hook. *Centre:* a gauge, two tambour hooks, a small hairpin. *Front row:* a steel crochet hook, a metal hook

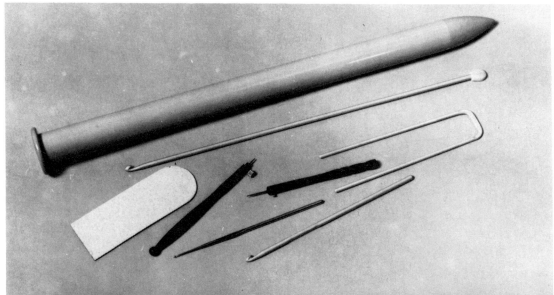

wool the ply refers to the number of strands woven. In the different makes of yarn each strand may vary in thickness so unless one is experienced it is wiser to use the yarn suggested in the pattern.

The basic method

To start a chain

The right hand holds the hook as for holding a pen and works the stitch *(diagram 1)*. The left hand is used to hold the work and to control the flow of the yarn and to keep the required tension.

A loop is now made and placed on the hook, which is held in the right hand *(diagrams 2 & 3)*.

The back of the left hand is held uppermost with the ball of yarn running freely from the left. The thread is passed between the little finger and the third finger, from the front to the back of the hand, then round the little finger to the front and across the back of the hand until reaching the loop on the hook. This loop is now held by the knot between the first finger and the thumb of the left hand *(diagram 4)*. The little finger can now be curled into the palm of the left hand to help regulate the flow of the yarn and the middle finger held raised to gently guide it.

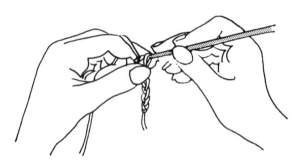

Diagram 1   Holding the hook

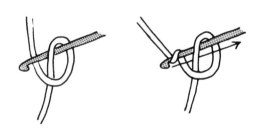

Diagrams 2 & 3   Making a loop

At this stage it is helpful to draw attention to the position of working. The elbows of the crochet worker should be held at each side of the body on a level with the hips. This makes for a relaxed position and avoids cramped neck muscles and tensed fingers. The hook should move through the stitches with a piston movement horizontally from right to left. Throughout the work the knot of the loop should always be held close under the hook, in order that the hands do not run away from each other.

Diagram 4   Holding the thread

Left-handed workers

Hold the hook between the thumb and the first finger of the left hand to make the first loop. Hold the base of the knot between the thumb and the first finger of the right hand. Hold the working yarn in the right hand taking it over the second finger, under the third finger and around the fourth finger. Raise the second finger so that the yarn is extended for the hook to pass under and over it. Use the second finger of the left hand to move the working loops up and down the hook as the work proceeds.

Method of working

Each row or round is worked from the left to right throughout. To follow instructions, read left for

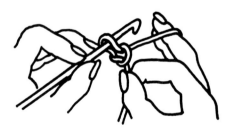

Diagram 5   Working for left-handed workers

right, and right for left. Place a mirror to the right of the diagram (at right angles) to reflect the illustration, and this will give the correct position for left-handed workers. Otherwise work exactly the same as for right-handed workers *(diagram 5)*.

To make the chain

Holding the yarn and the hook as originally explained, with the hook draw the yarn held in the left hand through the loop on the hook. This makes the first chain stitch *(diagram 1)*. Continue in this way for the required number of chain.

It is at this stage that one usually checks the tension of the work. If it is difficult to work the following row into this foundation row, then the tension is too tight and a larger size of hook must be used. If, however, a wavy line shows, then a smaller hook is used. The correct tension will come with practice.

To work the stitches

A double crochet

This is the shortest of all the stitches. Swing the chain to the left and work along the top edge, always by working under the top two strands. Put the hook into the second chain from the hook and catch the yarn on the hook. Draw a loop through and there will now be two loops on the hook *(diagram 6)*. Catch the yarn as before and draw it through both loops on the hook, leaving one loop; thus one double crochet is made. Repeat this movement along the row working in every chain *(diagram 7)*. For the second and all the following rows, after completing the last stitch work one chain before swinging the work once more to the left and repeat the first row *(figure 2)*.

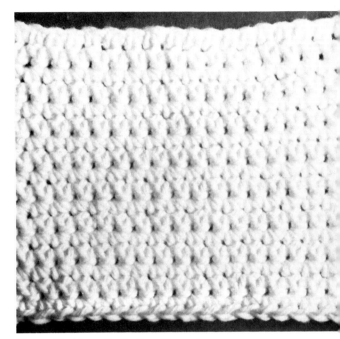

Fig. 2   Working a block of double crochet

A treble crochet

Make a length of chain as before and turn it to the left. Wind the yarn over the hook, miss the first two chain, not counting the loop on the hook. Insert the hook into the third chain, catch the yarn and pull through the loop on the hook. There will now be three loops on the hook *(diagram 8)*. Draw the yarn through the

Diagram 6   Commencing a double crochet

Diagram 7   Completing a double crochet

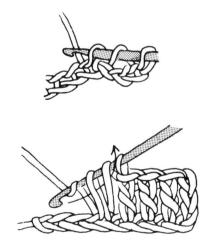

Diagram 8   Commencing a treble

11

first two loops, which will leave two loops on the hook *(diagram 9)*. Finally draw the yarn through the last two loops and this completes a treble crochet. Always work three chain before turning and starting a new row *(figure 3)*.

A half treble

Make a length of chain. Wind the yarn over the hook, miss two chain and insert the hook into the third chain as for the treble stitch and then catch the yarn through making three loops on the hook. Wind the yarn over the hook and pull through all the three loops *(diagram 10)*. This completes one half treble; repeat this movement into each chain stitch along the row, turning at the end with two chain.

A slip stitch

This stitch is used when forming a circle, or when casting off, or when moving from one part of a pattern to another where no depth of stitch is required *(diagram 11)*. With one loop on the hook, insert the hook into the next stitch to be used, catch the yarn and pull the loop through the stitch and the loop on the hook in one movement *(diagram 12)*.

A double treble

This stitch is worked in the same way as the treble, but the yarn is wound twice around the hook making

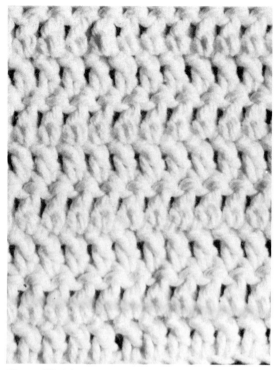

Fig. 3   Working a treble

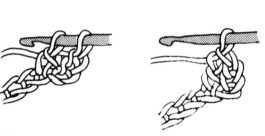

Diagram 9   Completing a treble

Diagram 11   Commencing a slip stitch
Diagram 12   Completing a slip stitch

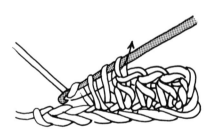

Diagram 10   Working a half treble

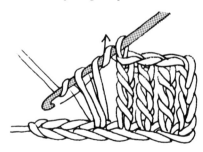

Diagram 13   Working a double treble

12

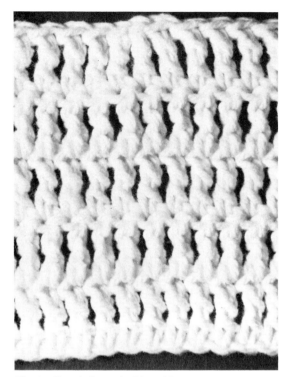

Fig. 4 Completing a double treble

Fig. 5 Working blocks and spaces

four loops on the hook *(diagram 13)*. After this each pair of loops are worked off until the last loop is left on the hook *(figure 4)*.

A triple treble

This is worked in the same way as the double treble, only the yarn is wound three times around the hook before taking off the following pairs of loops until only one remains on the hook.

A quadruple treble

Wind the yarn four times around the hook before working off each pair of loops until one remains on the hook.

A quintuple treble

Wind the yarn five times around the hook before working off each pair of loops until one remains on the hook.

Treble crochet groups

Blocks and spaces

Make a chain of 32 sts.

Row 1 1 tr in the 3rd ch from the hook, 1 tr in the next ch, * 3 ch, miss 3 ch, 1 tr in each of the next 3 ch; repeat from * ending with miss 3 ch, 1 tr into the last ch, 2 ch, turn.
Row 2 2 tr under the first 3 ch, * 3 ch, 3 tr under the next 3 ch; repeat from * ending with 3 ch, 1 tr into the top of the turning ch, 2 ch, turn.
Repeat Row 2 for the pattern *(figure 5)*.

Granny's square

4 ch, join with ss to form a ring.
Round 1 3 ch, 2 tr into the ring, * 3 ch, 3 tr into the ring; repeat from * twice more, 3 ch, join with ss to the top of 3 ch.
Round 2 3 ch, 2 tr into the same space, * 2 ch; in the next space work 3 tr, 3 ch, 3 tr; repeat from * twice more, 2 ch, 3 tr in the same space as the first 3 ch. Join with ss in the top of 3 ch.
Round 3 3 ch, 2 tr in the same space, * 2 ch, 3 tr in the next sp, 2 ch; in the corner space work 3 tr, 3 ch, 3 tr; repeat from * ending with 2 ch, 3 tr in the same sp as the first 3 ch, 3 ch, join with ss to the top of 3 ch.
Round 4 Repeat Round 3 only having 2 groups of 3 tr between the corners.

Fig. 6   Completing a granny's square

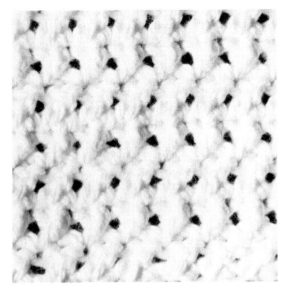

Fig. 7   Working crossed trebles

Round 5   Repeat Round 3 only having 3 groups of 3 tr between the corners *(figure 6)*.

Crossed trebles

Make 29 ch.

Row 1   Work 1 tr into 4th ch from the hook, and keeping the hook in the back of the last tr, work 1 tr in the 3rd ch from the hook, * miss 1 ch, 1 tr in the next ch, and from the back, work 1 tr in the missed st (crossed tr) repeat from * to the last ch, 1 tr into the last ch. 2 ch, turn.

Row 2   Miss the first tr, * work the crossed tr over the next 2 tr; repeat from * ending 1 tr in the top of the turning ch. 2 ch, turn.

Repeat Row 2 for the pattern *(figure 7)*.

Treble triangles

Make 30 ch.

Row 1   2 tr in 3rd ch from the hook, * miss 1 ch, 2 tr in the next ch; repeat from * ending with 1 tr in the last ch, 2 ch, turn.

Row 2   Work 2 tr in the sp between the trs of each 2 tr group of Row 1, ending with 1 tr in the top of the turning ch, 2 ch, turn.

Repeat Row 2 for the pattern *(figure 8)*.

Shell and openwork design

Shell

Make 29 ch

Row 1   1 dc into 2nd ch from the hook and in each chain to the end, 3 ch, turn.

Row 2   Miss the first 2 dc, * 5 tr into the next dc, miss 3 dc, repeat from * ending with miss 2 dc, 1 tr into the last dc, 1 ch, turn.

Row 3   1 dc in the first tr, 2 ch, 1 dc in the centre tr of the 5 tr group, * 3 ch, 1 dc in the centre tr of the next group; repeat from * ending with 2 ch, 1 dc in the top of the turning chain, 3 ch, turn.

Row 4   * 5 tr in the next dc; repeat from * ending with 1 tr in the last dc, 1 ch, turn.

Repeat Rows 2 and 3 for the pattern *(figure 9)*.

Split shell

Make 36 ch.

Row 1   1 dc into the first ch, * 4 ch, miss 3 ch, 1 dc into the next ch, repeat from * to the end of the row, 1 dc into the last ch, 4 ch, turn.

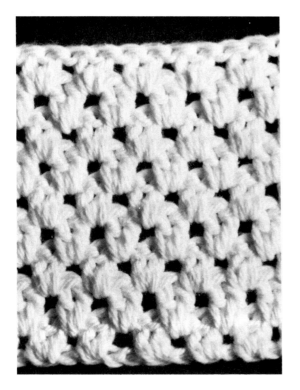

Fig. 8   Working treble triangles
Fig. 9   Completing a shell
Fig. 10   Working a split shell

Row 2   Miss 2 ch, 1 dc into the next ch, ★ 3 tr, 3 ch, 3 tr into the next ch, 1 dc into the next ch, 4 ch, 1 dc into the next ch; repeat from ★ ending with 1 dc into the last ch, 1 tr into the last dc, 1 ch, turn.

Row 3   1 dc into the first tr, ★4 ch, 1 dc 4 ch 1 dc, into the 3 ch loop, 4 ch, into the next 4 ch loop, repeat from ★ ending with 4 ch, 1 dc 4 ch, 1 dc into the next 3 ch loop, 4 ch, 1 dc into the 2nd of the turning chain, 4 ch, turn.

Repeat Rows 2 and 3 for the pattern *(figure 10)*.

Shell over shell

Make 30 ch.

Row 1   1 tr into the 7th ch from the hook, miss 2 ch, 5 tr into the next ch, ★ miss 2 ch, 1 tr into the next ch, miss 1 ch, 1 ch, 1 tr into the next ch, repeat from ★ to the end of the row, 4 ch, turn.

Fig. 11   Working shell over shell

Row 2   Miss 1 ch, 1 tr into the next tr, miss 2 tr, ★ 5 tr into the centre tr of the tr group of the previous row. 1 tr into the next tr, 1 ch, miss 1 ch, 1 tr into the next tr, repeat from ★ ending with 5 tr into the centre tr of the tr group of the previous row; 1 tr into the next tr, 1 ch, 1 tr into the 2nd of the turning ch. 4 ch, turn.

Repeat Row 2 for the pattern *(figure 11)*.

Solomon's knot

Commence with the required length of chain with a multiple of 6 ch plus 2

Row 1   1 dc into the 2nd chain from the hook, ★ draw the loop on the hook up 6 mm ($\frac{1}{4}$ in), thread over the hook and draw through the loop on the hook, insert the hook between the loop and the single thread of this chain and complete as dc (knot st made), work another knot in the same manner (a Solomon's knot made), miss 5 ch, 1 dc into the next ch; repeat from ★ ending with $1\frac{1}{2}$ Solomon's knots, turn.

Fig. 12   A Solomon's knot

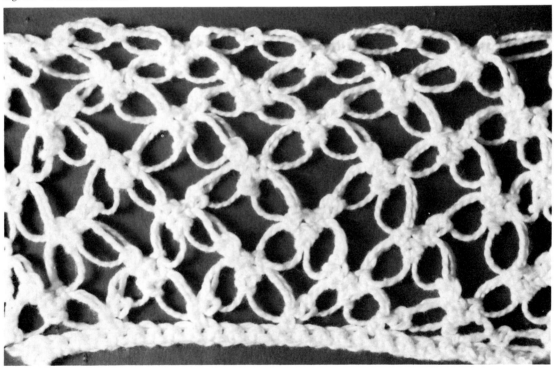

Row 2★   I dc over the double loop at the right of centre of the next knot, I dc over the double loop at the left of the same knot, I Solomon's knot; repeat from ★ omitting I Solomon's knot at the end of the last repeat, 1½ Solomon's knots. Turn.

Repeat Row 2 for the length required omitting 1½ Solomon's knots at the end of the last row *(figure 12)*.

Oyster stitch

Row 1   Make 25 ch, I dc into the 8th ch from the hook, ★ 5 ch, miss 3 ch, I dc into the next ch, 6 ch, miss 5 ch, I dc into the next ch, repeat from ★ along the row, ending after the last repeat with 5 ch, miss 3 ch, I dc into the next ch, 2 ch, miss 3 ch, I tr into the first ch, turn.

Row 2   I ch, I dc into the same ch, miss 2 ch, ★ 11 tr into the next 5 ch sp, I dc into the next 6 ch sp, and repeat from ★ along the row ending with 11 tr into the last 5 ch sp, I dc into the 3rd of the turning ch, turn.

Row 3   3 ch, miss 2 tr, ★ I tr, I ch, into the 3rd tr; I tr, I ch, into each of the next 5 tr, I tr into the next tr,

miss 2 tr, I dc, and 2 tr; repeat from ★ to the end of the row, ending with I dbl tr into the last dc, turn.

Row 4   I ch, I dc into the dbl tr, I ch, I dc into the next ch, ★ 3 ch, I dc into the next ch, repeat from ★ 4 more times, ending with I ch, I dc between the two groups of tr, repeat from the beginning along the row, ending with I dc into the first of the turning ch, turn with 6 ch.

Row 5   I dc into the 2nd pct, 5 ch, I dc into the 4th pct, repeat along the row.

Repeat Rows 2 to 4 inclusive for pattern *(figure 13)*.

Fan stitch

Make 37 ch.

Row 1   I dc into the 2nd ch from the hook, ★ I ch, miss 4 ch, (I dbl tr 2 ch) 4 times into the next ch, I dbl tr into the same place, I ch, miss 4 ch, I dc into the next ch, repeat from ★ to the last repeat, ending with I ch, miss 4 ch, I dbl tr, 2 ch, I dbl tr, 2 ch, I dbl tr into the first of the foundation ch, turn.

Fig. 13   An oyster stitch

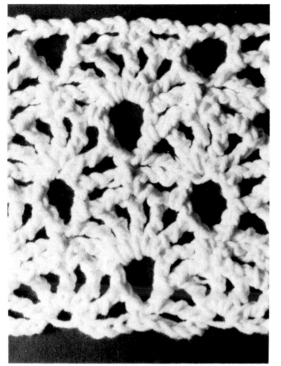

Fig. 14   A fan stitch

Fig. 15   A block of seed stitch

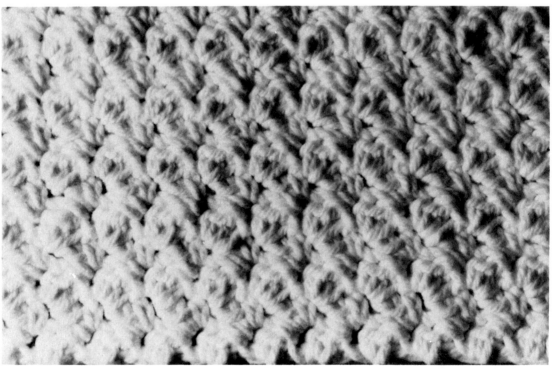

Fig. 16   Crazy shell

Row 2 1 ch, 1 dc into the last dbl tr, 3 ch; 1 tr into the 2nd 2 ch sp, 2 ch, * 1 tr into the first 2 ch sp of the next group, 3 ch, miss 1 dbl tr, 2 ch; 1 dc into the next dbl tr, 3 ch, miss 2 ch, 1 tr into the next 2 ch sp, 2 ch, repeat from * ending with 1 ch instead of 2 ch, miss last dbl tr, 1 ch, 1 dbl tr into the last dc. Turn.

Row 3 7 ch, into the first ch work 1 dbl tr, 2 ch, 1 dbl tr, 1 ch; * 1 dc into the first dc, into the next 2 ch sp work (1 dbl tr, 2 ch) 4 times, 1 dbl tr, 1 ch into the same space; repeat from * along the row ending with 1 dc into the turning ch, 5 ch, turn.

Row 4 *1 tr into the first 2 ch sp, 3 ch, miss 2 ch; 1 dc into the centre dbl tr, 3 ch, miss 2 ch, and 1 dbl tr; 1 tr into the last 2 ch sp, 2 ch; repeat from * along the row, ending with 1 ch, turn.

Repeat Rows 1 to 4 for the pattern *(figure 14)*.

Seed stitch

Make an even number of ch.

Row 1 2 dc in the 2nd ch from the hook, * miss 1 ch, 2 dc in the next ch; repeat from * to the end of the row, 2 ch, turn.

Row 2 * miss the first dc, 2 dc in the next dc; repeat from * ending 1 dc in the top of the turning chain, 2 ch, turn.

Repeat Row 2 for the pattern *(figure 15)*.

Crazy shell

Make 36 ch.

Row 1 2 tr into the 3rd ch from the hook, * miss 2 ch, 1 dc and 2 tr in the next ch; repeat from * ending with 2 ch, 1 dc in the last chain, 2 ch, turn.

Row 2 2 tr in the first dc, * miss 2 tr, 1 dc and 2 tr in the next dc; repeat from * ending 1 dc in the top of the turning chain, 2 ch, turn.

Repeat Row 2 for the pattern *(figure 16)*.

A Victorian mat

Make 12 chain and join with ss to form a ring, 3 ch.

Row 1 Make 23 tr into the ring, join with ss into the top of the first tr, 6 ch.

Row 2 1 tr into the next tr, * 2 ch, 1 tr into the next tr, repeat from * all round, ending with 2 ch, ss into the 4th of the 6 ch.

Row 3 12 ch, miss 1 tr, 1 dbl tr into the next tr, * 8 ch, miss 1 tr, 1 dbl tr into the next tr; repeat from * all round, ending with 8 ch, ss into 4th of 12 ch.

Row 4 6 ch, 4 tr into the next 8 ch loop, * 3 ch, 1 dbl tr into the next dbl tr, 3 ch, 4 tr into the next 8 ch loop;

repeat from * ending with 3 ch, ss into the 4th of 6 ch.

Row 5 8 ch, 1 dbl tr into the last ss, * 4 ch, 1 tr into each of the next 4 tr, 4 ch, 1 dbl tr into the next dbl tr, 4 ch, 1 dbl tr into the *same* dbl tr; repeat from * ending with 4 ch, 1 tr into *each* of the next 4 tr; 4 ch, ss into the 4th of the 8 ch.

Row 6 8 ch, 4 dbl tr into the next 4 ch sp; * 6 ch, miss 2 tr, into the next tr, 6 ch, miss 1 tr, 5 dbl tr into the next 4 ch sp, repeat from * all round, ending with 6 ch, miss 1 tr, 2 tr into the next tr; 6 ch, 1 ss into the top of the first 6 ch.

Row 7 1 ch, 1 dc into each of the next 4 dbl tr, * 8 ch, miss 1 tr, 1 trip tr into the next tr, 8 ch, 1 dc into each of the next 5 dbl tr; repeat from * all round, ending with 8 ch, miss 1 tr, 1 trip tr into the next tr, 8 ch, 1 ss into the first dc.

Row 8 1 dc into each of the next 4 dc, * 6 dc into the next 8 ch loop, 1 dc into the next trip tr, 6 dc into the next 8 ch loop, 1 dc into the next 5 dc, repeat from * all round ending with 6 dc into the next 8 ch loop; 1 ss into the first dc.

Row 9 3 ch, miss 1 dc, 1 hlf tr into the next dc; * 1 ch, 1 hlf tr into the next dc; repeat from * all round, 1 ss into the first hlf tr, (108 sps).

Row 10 1 ss into each of the next chain and hlf tr; 3 ch, 2 tr into the next 1 ch sp, 1 tr into the next hlf tr; * 10 ch, miss 4 sps, 1 dbl tr into the next hlf tr, 5 ch, 1 dbl tr into the same hlf tr as previous dbl tr, 10 ch, miss 4 sps, 1 tr into next hlf tr, 2 tr into the next sp, 1 tr into the next hlf tr, rep from * all round, ending with 10 ch, 1 dbl tr into the next hlf tr, 5 ch, 1 dbl tr into the same hlf tr as before, 10 ch, 1 ss into the top of the 3 ch.

Row 11 ss into the first 2 tr; 1 tr into the same tr, 6 ch, 1 dc into the next 10 ch sp; 5 ch. Into the next 5 ch sp (between the 2 dbl tr) work * a 3 dbl tr cl (leaving the last loop of each on the hook) then draw through all loops on the hook, 2 ch; repeat from * 3 times more; 5 ch, 1 dc into the 10 ch loop, 5 ch, miss 1 tr, 1 tr into each of next 2 tr, miss 1 tr, 5 ch, 1 dc into the next 10 ch loop, 5 ch, then leaving the last loop of each on the hook and draw through all the loops work into the next 5 ch loop (a 3 dbl tr cl, 2 ch) 3 times and a 3 dbl tr cl; repeat from * all round ending with 5 ch, 1 dc into the 10 ch loop, 5 ch, 1 ss into the top of the 3 ch.

Row 12 1 ch, 1 dc into the same space, * 4 ch, miss the next 5 ch loop; into the next 5 ch loop work 1 dbl tr 3 ch, 1 dbl tr; then into next 2 ch sp work (1 dbl tr, 3 ch, 1 dbl tr) 3 times, 1 dbl tr, 3 ch, 1 dbl tr into the next 5 ch sp, 4 ch, miss 1 tr, 1 dc into the next tr; repeat from * all round, omitting 1 dc at the end of the last repeat and ending with 1 ss into the first dc.

Fig. 17   A Victorian mat

Row 13 1 ch, 1 dc into the same sp, * 3 ch, (2 tr, 5 ch into the next 3 ch sp) 5 times, 3 ch, 1 dc into the next dc, repeat from * all round omitting 1 dc at the end of the last repeat, ss in first dc.

Row 14 1 ch, * 3 dc into the next 3 ch loop; (2 dc, 2 ch, 2 dc, 2 ch, 2 dc, 2 ch, 2 dc into the next 5 ch loop) 4 times; 3 dc into the next 3 ch loop; 1 dc into the next dc; repeat from * all round. Fasten off *(figure 17)*.

A mat from Cyprus

Materials
Plastic rings 19 mm ($\frac{3}{4}$ in) outside diameter
Cotton No. 10, Croknit silk or Lizbett, small quantity in yellow, white and dark jade green
Hook 2.50 or 2.00
Measurements
Size of mat: 23 × 23 cm (9 × 9 in)

Diagram 14   Completing the first motif

To work over plastic ring

Work 24 dc into ring making 1 picot every 6th dc (picot is make 6 dc, 4 ch, 6 dc) ss to join. Fasten off.

First motif

Round 1   With yellow work 25 dc, ss to join.
Round 2   Join on white and work 1 dc into ss, work 14 ch, 1 dc into 2nd dc on centre; 7 ch, 1 ss into 7th ch prior to last dc, 7 ch, 1 dc into next dc on centre. (1 ch cluster made) work 11 more clusters (12).
Round 3   Join on jade green with 1 dc. Into tip of any petal, * work 12 ch, 1 dc. Into tip of next petal, repeat from * all round, ss into 1st dc.
Round 4   Work * 5 dc into first ch sp, 4 ch, 5 dc into same sp, 1 dc into tip of next petal. Repeat from * all round. Join any picot of first motif to first picot on ring *(diagram 14)*.

Second motif

Work rows 1, 2 and 3 of the first motif.
   Complete two chain spaces, join picots at next free picot on ring, finish two more chain loops, join on a second ring at any picot, complete second motif leaving last two chain loops for joining to first motif at corresponding two chain loops *(diagram 15)*.

Diagram 15   Joining the first and the second motif to a ring picot

Third motif

Complete three rows as before and join at next free picot on ring and complete fourth row by joining picots of last two chain loops to corresponding two picots on second motif *(diagram 16)*.

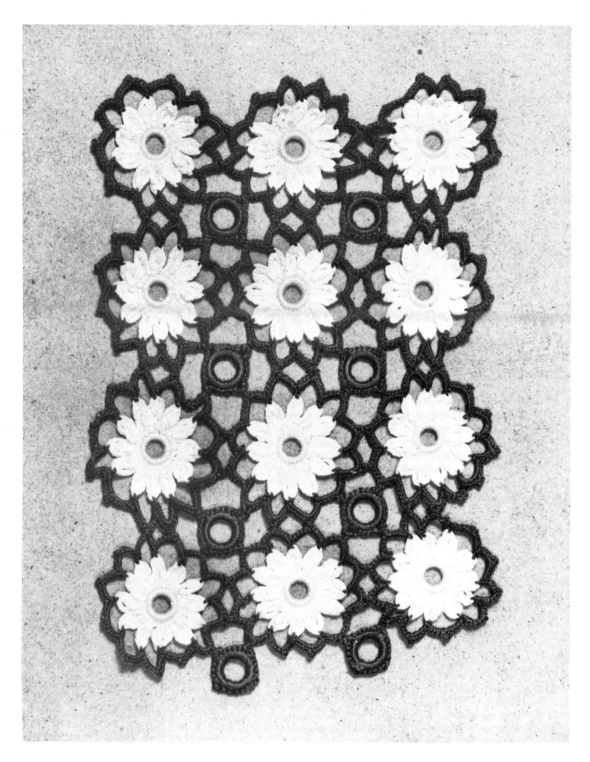

Fig. 18   A Cyprus daisy mat

22

Fourth motif

Complete Rows 1 to 3 as before.

Round 4 Join first and second picots to last two chain loops of third motif. Join next picot of fourth motif to remaining picot on ring. The next two picots are joined to the two corresponding picots of first motif *(diagram 17)*.

The next motif is worked in the same way, always joining at corresponding picots and adding a new ring where required. There should be joins at every chain loop and all ring picots should be joined to motifs *(figure 18)*.

Diagram 16   Joining the third motif to picots

Diagram 17   Completing the joining of all motifs and rings

2 BOSNIAN CROCHET

Historical background

Bosnia is a province in Yugoslavia, and this form of crochet is peculiar to the region. It resembles peasant weaving and in appearance it is akin to American Indian needlepoint. In the designs bold colours are used, dark blues, greens and rust-red on plain backgrounds predominating.

Two methods are used. One uses only the forward row with the threads being cut at the end of the row, joining on the thread at the beginning of the following row on starting again; the other method works with a double crochet and turns at the end of every row.

Diagram 18   Working a slip stitch through the front of a stitch. When completing a slip stitch row the ends are cut
Diagram 19   Working into the back of the stitch

The designs are chiefly geometric or stylised birds, animals, or flowers. To achieve a clear outline to the pattern, a firm, smooth thread must be used, and the patterns of both cross stitch and tapestry can be studied.

The two methods

In Bosnian crochet there is a choice of two methods to achieve the flat and firm surface necessary for the designs. The first step is to trace the chosen pattern onto squared paper and then the design is followed from it, taking each square to represent a stitch.

To work method 1

This is the traditional method when a slip stitch is used *(diagram 18)*. The work is not turned at the end of the row, but the thread is cut leaving a short end,

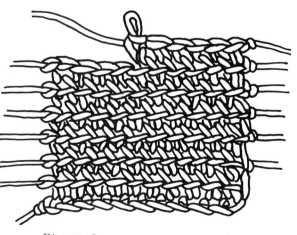

Diagram 18

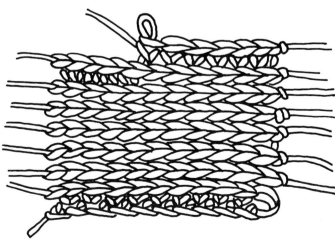

Diagram 19

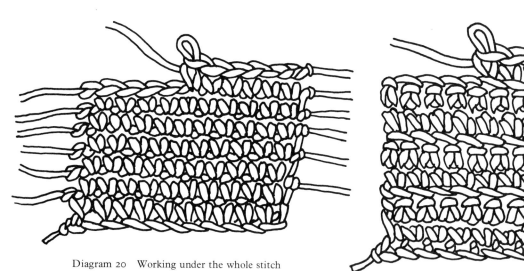

Diagram 20   Working under the whole stitch

Diagram 22   Working a double crochet into the back of a stitch

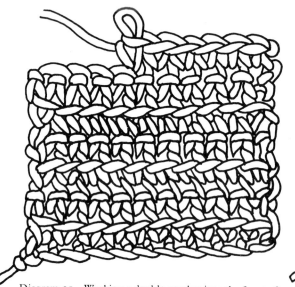

Diagram 21   Working a double crochet into the front of a stitch

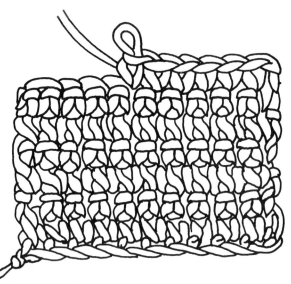

Diagram 23   Working a double crochet under a whole stitch

which is later darned along the stitches at the back of the work. The thread is joined on again at the beginning of the next row. The pattern of the squares is followed for the remainder of the design.

This pattern may be varied by inserting the hook through the back *(diagram 19)* or the front of the stitch when making the slip stitch, or under the complete stitch to emphasise the three-dimensional effect of the design. At the completion of the pattern, turn the work and thread away the ends *(diagram 20)*.

To work method 2

A double crochet is used here instead of the slip stitch and as in basic crochet the work is turned at the end of the row. Once again, as in method 1, the effect can be varied by the introduction of another colour against the main background. The choice can be made of working into the front of the stitch, into the back of the stitch or under the whole stitch *(diagrams 21, 22 & 23)*.

To work a pattern of alternate back and front stitches

Make a chain measuring the length required for the project.

Row 1 Insert the hook into the second chain, y o h, and pull the thread through, put the hook in the next chain, y o h, and pull the loop through the two loops on the hook. Continue to work this slip stitch to the end of the row, cut the thread and pull this through the last loop.

Row 2 Join on the thread at the beginning of the next row. Insert the hook into the back of the second stitch, y o h, and pull through as a slip stitch. Repeat this slip stitch into the following two stitches. Insert the hook into the front of the next stitch, y o h, pull through the two loops on the hook. Continue in this way along the row, one stitch into the back of each of the next three stitches, followed by one stitch into the front of each of the next two stitches *(diagrams 18 & 19)*.

The following designs are suitable for braids, belts or bags *(diagrams 24, 25 & 26)*.

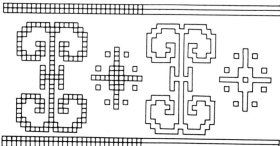

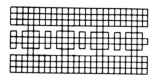

Diagrams 24, 25 & 26 Designs suitable for braids, belts or bag flaps

3 BROOMSTICK CROCHET

This is one of the modern techniques, which uses the combination of knitting and crochet to make the open loop effect.

It is known also by other names (jiffy lace, whizz-pin lace) but broomstick is most commonly used to refer to the large knitting pin. During the last ten years it has been very popular in the USA, where many new designs and techniques are being successful, and the last few years have seen its popularity grow in the UK *(diagram 27)*.

This craft lends itself to the making of garments with an open lacey effect in either very fine yarns, or the bulky yarns which have proved so fashionable of recent years. The technique is still in its infancy, but should soon show many exciting new stitches.

The basic method

The knitting needle is held in the left hand with an overhand grip, with the crochet hook held in the right hand as one would hold a pen *(diagram 28)*.

Using the crochet hook and the yarn make a chain for the required length.

Row 1 With the hook lift up the last loop of the chain and place this on the knitting needle. Repeat this movement into each stitch of the chain until all the stitches have been picked up and these should number the same as the cast on chain *(diagrams 29 & 30)*.

Row 2 * Insert the hook through the centre of the first five loops on the knitting needle. This number

Diagram 27   A broomstick needle

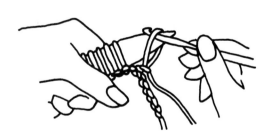

Diagram 28   Holding the needle

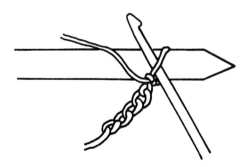

Diagram 29   Lifting up the last loop onto the needle

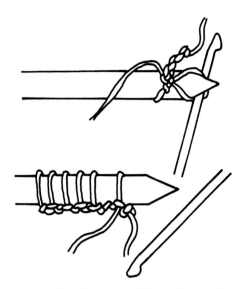

Diagram 30   Completing the stitches on the needle

Diagram 31   Working off the loops for the patterns

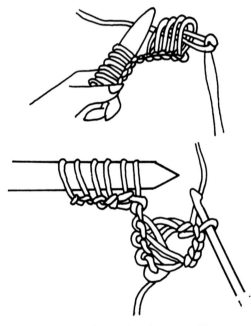

Diagrams 32 & 33   Completing the group of loops

will vary according to the pattern *(diagram 31)*. Hold these stitches together as one stitch, y o h, pull through all five loops and slip the group from the needle. Work five dc into this same group *(diagrams 32 & 33)* and repeat from * along the row. Do not turn work.

Repeat Rows 1 and 2 for the pattern.

Horizontal groups

To work a classic sleeveless cardigan

Materials
Double knitting yarn 10 × 20 g balls (8 oz)
A broomstick No. 25 mm (1 in)
A crochet hook No. 4.50 mm
Measurements
To fit bust 87 mm (34 in)
Tension
1 group to 2.5 cm (1 in) in width

The main part

This is worked in one piece up to the underarms.
With the crochet hook cast on 171 stitches.
Row 1 Pull up the last loop and place it on the knitting needle. Insert the hook in each remaining stitch of the chain, pull the yarn through and place it on the needle (171 stitches).
Row 2 Draw the yarn through the first 5 loops, 1 ch (5 dc in 5 loops together) to the end.
Rows 1 to 2 form the pattern. Repeat these seven times, and Row 1.

To work the front shaping

Next Row 1 ch, work as Row 2 over 35 dc, turn. Continue on these stitches only.
Pattern another four rows.
Next row Pattern to last 5 loops, 3 dc in 5 loops together.
Next row Pattern to the end of the row.
Next row Pattern to last 8 loops, 3 dc in 8 loops together.
Next row Pattern to the end of the row.
Next row Pattern to the last 8 loops, 5 dc in 8 loops together.
Pattern two rows. Fasten off. Miss next 14 dc of the main part (for first armhole), join yarn to the next dc and work as the first row over the following 70 stitches. Turn.
Pattern 11 rows on these stitches for the back. Fasten off. Miss next 14 dc of the main part (second armhole), join the yarn to the next dc, and work as

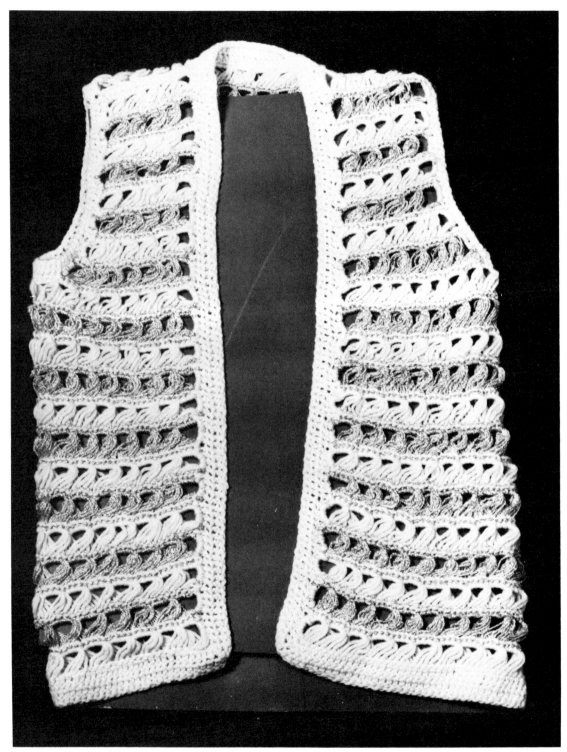

Fig. 19 A classic cardigan

row 2 over the last 35 dc.
Pattern 4 rows.

Next row 1 ch, 3 dc in 5 loops tog, pattern to the end.

Next row Pattern to the end.

Next row 1 ch, 3 dc in 8 loops tog, pattern to the end.

Next row Pattern to the end.

Next row 5 dc in 8 loops tog, pattern to the end. pattern two rows. Fasten off.

To make up the garment

Press the work. Join the shoulder seams. Work 1 dc in each chain along the lower edge and 4 dc in the side of each group of loops around the outer edge. Finish the armholes to match *(figure 19)*.

Vertical groups

Materials
3 × 20 g balls (2 oz) 2-ply yarn
Crochet hook 3.00 mm
Broomstick No. 12 ($\frac{1}{2}$ in)
Measurements
Bust 83 cm (32$\frac{1}{2}$ in)
Tension
2 groups to 2.5 cm (1 in) in width
2 patterns to 3.8 cm (1$\frac{1}{2}$ in)

To work the main part

Make 85 ch loosely.

Foundation Row Miss 1 ch, 1 dc in each chain to the end.

Row 1 1 ch, 1 dc in the next stitch, draw up a loop, and place on the needle, (draw yarn through the next st 1 ch, draw up a loop and place on the needle) to the end.

Row 2 Draw yarn through the first 4 loops, 1 ch, 4 dc in these 4 loops together; (4 dc in 4 loops together) to the end.
Rows 1 and 2 form the pattern.

Neck shaping

Next row 1 ch, pattern to within last 4 dc, 2 loop sts in each of last 4 dc, (increase worked).
Increase at end of following two alternate rows.

Next row Make 21 ch; miss 1 ch, 1 dc in 20 ch; pattern to the end.
Pattern 8 rows.

Armhole shaping

Next row * Pattern over 64 dc, (miss 1 dc, loop st in next dc) 4 times (dec. worked) Turn. Continue on these sts.
Decrease at end of following alternate row.
Pattern seven rows.
Increase at end of next and following alternate row.

Next row Make 45 ch, miss 1 ch, dc in 44 ch, pattern to end *.
Pattern 30 rows. Repeat from * to *.
Pattern eight rows.

Neck shaping

Next row Pattern over 88 dc; dec, turn. Dec at beginning of next two alternate rows.
Pattern three rows. Fasten off.

To make up

Press lightly. Join the shoulder seams.

Edging 1 ch, 1 dc in each dc or 4 dc in side of the loop rows around the outer edge and armholes.

To work broomstick lace with a puff stitch

Make the required number of stitches for the chain.

Row 1 Insert the crochet hook in each stitch, pull the yarn through and place on the needle.

Row 2 Insert the hook in the centre of the first 3 loops, holding these loops together as one, y o h, and take off the needle, 1 ch, * dc, half tr, dc, half tr, dc, (popcorn), repeat from * into each group of 3 loops across the row. Do not turn.

Row 3 Insert the needle in the back of each stitch, pull yarn through, and place on the needle.
Repeat Rows 2 and 3 for the pattern.

To work with a single thread

Make the required number of chain.

Foundation Row Miss 1 ch, 1 dc in each ch to the end.

Row 1 1 ch, 1 dc in the next stitch; draw up a loop and place it on the needle (draw yarn through the next stitch, 1 ch, draw up the loop and place it on the needle) repeat this to the end of the row.

Row 2 Draw up yarn through the first loop on the needle, 1 ch, 1 dc in the same loop. Repeat into each dc to the end of the row.

A square design

Each Motif is 12.5 cm (5 in).
Materials
Knitting yarn
1 knitting needle
1 crochet hook

Row 1   With the crochet hook make 36 chain. Pull up the last loop and place it on the knitting needle, insert the hook into each stitch of the chain and place it on the needle.

Row 2   Insert the hook through all the first 3 loops, holding the loops together as 1 stitch, y o h, and take off the needle, 1 ch work 3 dc into this group of 3 loops, * work (3 dc, 3 ch, 3 dc) all into the next group of 3 loops, to make a corner; (3 dc in the next 3 loops) twice, repeat from * twice, then work corner pattern in the next set of 3 loops; 3 dc in next group of 3 loops. Fasten off and do not turn.

Row 3   Insert the hook into the back loop of the last dc; y o h, and pull the loop through the dc and place it on the needle, pull up a loop in the back loop of each dc and each chain stitch at the corner and place it on the needle (60 loops).

Row 4   Work (3 dc in next group of 3 loops) twice, * (2 dc, 3 half treble, 2 dc) all in the next group of 3 loops to make a corner, (3 dc in the next group of 3 loops) 4 times, repeat from * twice, work the corner pattern in the next group of 3 loops, (3 dc into the next group of 3 loops) twice, fasten off.

To work the centre

Thread a large-eyed needle with the yarn and from the right side of the work weave the needle through a single loop of each chain stitch of the foundation chain, draw up the stitches tightly and fasten off on the wrong side. Fasten the ends of the row together on the wrong side.

To work the border

With the right side facing, join the yarn to the centre dc of the second pattern before any corner, 3 ch, (counts as the first tr) 1 tr in the same st, 1 ch, 2 tr in the centre dc of the next pattern 1 ch, * 2 tr in the second st of the corner pattern, 1 ch, miss the next st, (1 tr, 3 ch, 1 tr) in the next stitch (corner) 1 ch, miss the next st, 2 tr in the next st, (2 tr in the centre dc of the next pattern, 1 ch) 4 times, repeat from * twice, work around corner pattern as before, (2 tr in the centre dc of the next pattern, 1 ch) twice; join with slip stitch in the top of 3 ch. Fasten off *(figure 20)*.

Fig. 20   A circle turned into a square

Making a circle

Each circle is 12.5 cm (5 in) with a border.
Materials
Knitting yarn
1 knitting needle
1 crochet hook
With the crochet hook and the yarn cast on 30 stitches for the chain.

Row 1   With the crochet hook pull up the last loop and place it on the knitting needle, * insert the hook in the next ch, pull the yarn through and place it on the needle, repeat from * across the row (30 loops).

Row 2   Insert the hook through the first 3 loops, holding the loops together as one loop, y o h, take through the group and off the needle, 1 ch, work (1 dc, 1 ch) 3 times in the first group of 3 loops, * work (1 dc, 1 ch) 3 times in all the next group of 3 loops, repeat from * across the row to the last group of 3 loops; in the last group work (1 dc, 1 ch) twice, 2 dc in the same space (10 patterns). Fasten off.

Row 3   On the right side, insert the hook in the back loop of the last dc, y o h, draw the loop through the dc and place it on the needle, * Draw up a loop in the

back loop of each ch and each dc and place it on the needle, repeat from * across the row (60 loops).

Row 4 Repeat Row 2 (20 patterns) Fasten off.

To form the centre

Attach the yarn on the right side in the single loop of the 1st ch on the foundation row, 3 ch, * y o h, insert the hook in the next ch, y o h, and draw up a loop, y o h, and through 2 loops, repeat from * across, holding the last loop of each stitch on the hook, y o h, and take through all the loops on the hook, draw up tightly, 1 ch, to hold.

Fasten off; join ends of the row to form a circle.

To work into a square

On the right side attach the yarn to centre dc of any pattern, 1 dc in the same stitch, * 5 ch, 1 dc in the centre dc of the next pattern, repeat from * around motif, 5 ch; join with a slip stitch in the first dc. Fasten off *(figure 21)*.

Fig. 21   A broomstick circle

4 CONTINENTAL LOOPING

Under this name there are two branches of the craft. In the older of them one crochets with yarn over a smooth, flat-surfaced tool, in this case a gauge, which is described in the following chapter. This type of crochet is used for shawls, garments and covers. The second branch of the craft uses the same method, but the material employed is cotton reminiscent of netting, which it imitates.

Tools

A crochet hook
Gauges of varying depth
Yarn or cotton

To make a gauge

It is necessary that one is able to make this, because at the moment it is not marketed.

Materials

Formica, clear perspex, plastic or cardboard of 2.25 mm (3/32nd in) in thickness. Gauges are used in the following widths: 6 mm ($\frac{1}{4}$ in); 13 mm ($\frac{1}{2}$ in); 19 mm ($\frac{3}{4}$ in); 2.5 cm (1 in); 4 cm ($1\frac{1}{2}$ in); 5 cm (2 in) and 6 cm ($2\frac{1}{2}$ in). Apart from using one for fringes, larger than the above measurements are seldom used as this would make a clumsy design.

To cut the gauge

Having drawn the shape on to tracing paper, carefully cut around the outline and place this on the perspex or cardboard. Then trace around this outline and with a fine-tooth saw or hacksaw cut around the material. Round off the ends and file off any sharp edges; rub them down with a file and finish with glass paper to make the gauge smooth.

The basic method

With the hook and the yarn make a chain of the required length and, still holding the hook in the right hand and the gauge in the space between the thumb and the first finger of the left hand, start to

Diagram 34   Examples of gauge sizes

work from right to left. Lift the last loop of the chain on to the gauge and the chain will then hang across the front of the gauge; the hook lies horizontally to the top of the gauge *(diagram 35)*. Do not remove the hook.

The yarn is now hanging at the back of the gauge. Pass the yarn loosely twice around the gauge from back to front. With one stitch already on the hook, insert the hook in the second chain from the hook; continue with the hook under the first wind on the gauge and pull the yarn of the last wind through all loops except the last. There are now two loops on the hook y o h; pull through the last two loops to complete the dc. Continue in this way until every chain has been used *(diagram 36)*.

Having reached the end of the row slip the loops from the gauge, turn the work upside down and make a chain equivalent to the depth of the gauge *(diagram 37)*. Next work a slip stitch into each loop to the end of the row. Lift the last loop back on to the gauge and repeat the forward row as before. Continue in the chosen pattern *(diagram 38 & 39)*.

The second method is a variation of working the groups of loops and is usually worked with cotton for tray cloths and mats, and for the single loops a double crochet is used as in the previous method.

Examples are shown in *diagrams 40, 41, 42, 43 & 44.*

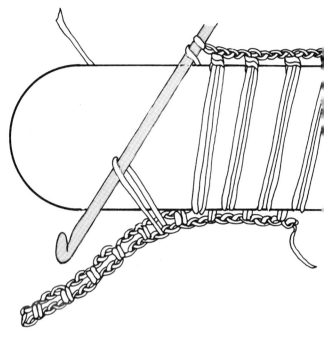

Diagram 35   Winding the yarn over the gauge

Loop groups

Tulip

Make the required number of chain, turn.
Row 1   Work 1 dc into the 8th ch, miss 4 ch, 1 dc into the next ch; repeat from * to the end of the row, 6 ch, turn.

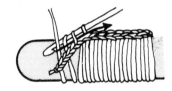

Diagram 36   Using all the loops of the chain

Row 2   Work 1 dc into the first chain loop, and repeat 6 ch, 1 dc into the next chain loop, to the end of the row, 6 ch, turn.
Row 3   With the gauge work a double loop st into the first chain loop; then * work a double loop st into the next chain loop, 2 ch, repeat from * to the end of the row, 6 ch, turn.
Row 4   Repeat Row 2 once.
Row 5   With the larger gauge 5 cm (2 in) and the crochet hook work into the first chain loop, 1 single loop st; then into the next chain loop work (single loop st, 2 ch) 4 times, miss 1 chain loop; work a single loop st into the next chain loop, joining it to the top of the last single loop st. * Into the same chain loop work

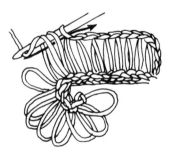

Diagram 37   Slipping the loops from the gauge

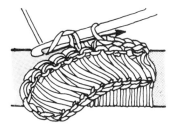

Diagram 38   Return slip stitch row

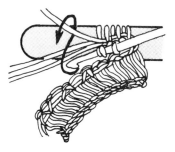

Diagram 39   The repeat of forward row

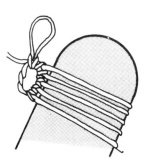

Diagram 40   Working several single loops
into one chain

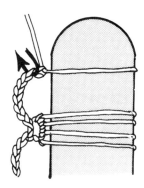

Diagram 41   Working alternate rings with chains

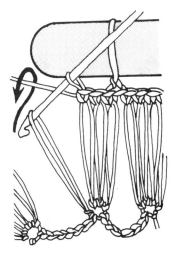

Diagram 42   Working a dc row into the row of loops

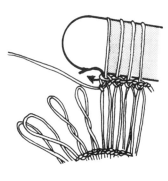

Diagram 43   Working alternate rows of loops and dc

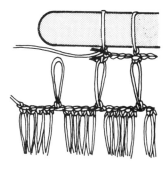

Diagram 44   Working spaced loops

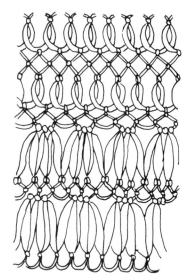

Diagram 45   Tulip design adapted from netting

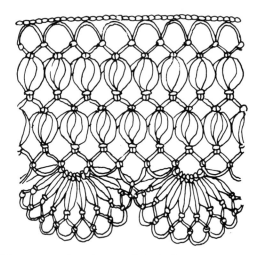

Diagram 46   Gooseberry and fan design

3 single loop st, 2 ch; repeat from ★ to the end of the row, 4 ch turn.

Row 6   1 dc into the first loop st, 3 ch, ★ 1 dc into the next loop st, 3 ch, and repeat from ★ to the end of the row.

Row 7   Repeat Row 6.

Row 8   1 dc into the top of each loop st with 4 ch between each loop (*diagram 45*).

Repeat Rows 2 to 8 for the pattern.

Gooseberry and fan

With the crochet hook and yarn make the required number of chain.

Row 1   Work 1 dc into the 4th ch from the hook, 1 dc into the next ch, ★ 6 ch, miss 4 ch, 1 dc into the next ch; repeat from ★ to the end of the row, 6 ch, turn.

Row 2   Repeat Row 1.

Row 3   With the gauge make a 2 double loop st group in the first chain loop, ★ 4 ch, 2 double loop st group in the next chain loop; repeat from ★ to the end of the row.

Row 4   Repeat Row 1.

Row 5   Repeat Row 3.

Row 6   Repeat Row 1.

Row 7   Repeat Row 6.

Row 8   1 dc into the first chain loop, miss 1 chain loop, ★ into the next chain loop work 8 double loop sts, with 4 ch between each pair. miss 1 chain loop, 4 ch, 1 dc into the next chain loop, 4 ch; repeat from ★ to the end of the row.

Row 9   Repeat Row 1 (*diagram 46*).

Lantern

With the crochet hook and yarn make the required number of chain.

Row 1   Into the 4th ch work 1 dc. ★ 6 ch, miss 4 ch, 1 dc into the next ch, repeat from ★ to the end of the row.

Row 2   With the hook and the gauge work 2 loop sts into the first chain loop, 2 ch, 1 single loop st back into the same chain loop, ★ 1 single loop st into dc of next chain loop, 2 ch, 2 single loop st into same chain loop, 2 ch, 1 single loop st into the same chain loop; repeat from ★ to the end of the row.

Row 3   2 single loop st into the first st, miss 2 ch, ★ 1 single loop st into each of the next 2 loop st of the previous row, miss 2 ch, 1 single loop st into the next dc 4 ch, 1 single loop st into the last dc miss 2 ch, repeat from ★ to the end of the row (*diagram 47*).

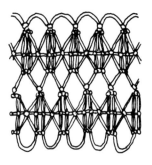

Diagram 47   Lantern design

38

A cape in simple loop stitch

Materials

7 × 25 g (6 oz) balls of Gossamer Mohair

Gauge 5 cm (2 in)

Hook 3.50 mm

Measurements

Centre of the neck to the hem   50 cm (20 in)

Around the hem   160 cm (64 in)

Around the neck   70 cm (28 in)

Length of the ties   30 cm (12 in)

To begin the cape

Foundation chain   With the crochet hook and yarn make a chain of 104 st, 1 half tr into the 3rd ch from the hook, * 1 ch, miss the next ch, 1 half tr into the following ch, repeat from * along the row increasing evenly across the row eight times by working 1 half tr, 1 ch, 1 half tr into the same stitch.

Row 1   (Loop stitch row). Place markers at each increase on the loop row; using the gauge work a double loop stitch into each space of previous row, and increase into the centre space and into the fourth space either side of the centre. Continue to the end of the row, 6 ch, turn.

Row 2   Repeat the half tr row, as in the foundation row, increasing evenly five times across the row as before.

Row 3   Work a row of loop stitches as in Row 1, working an increase on each side of the centre and on the eighth st each side of the centre.

Fig. 22   A shawl with a petal and bud design

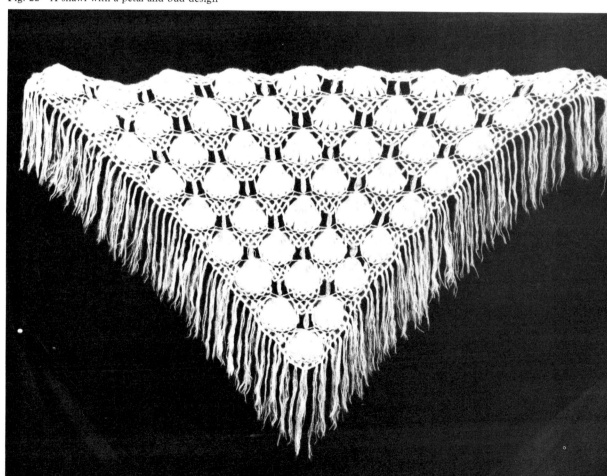

39

Fig. 23   A section of the shawl

Row 4   Work a half tr row as before, working 7 increase evenly across the row.

Row 5   Work a loop st row making 3 increases evenly across the row.

Row 6   Work the half tr row increasing 7 times evenly across the row.

Row 7   Work the loop st row increasing evenly 5 times across the row.

Row 8   Work the half tr space row but increase 7 times evenly across the row.

Row 9   Work the loop st row increasing 5 times evenly across the row.

Row 10   Work the half tr space row with 7 increases evenly across the row.

Row 11   Work the loop st row with increasing 7

times across the row.

Row 12   Work the half tr row with 10 increases spaced evenly across the row.

Row 13   Work the loop st row with increasing 4 times evenly across the row.

Row 14   Work the half tr row with 7 increasings evenly across the row.

Row 15   Work the loop st row increasing 5 times evenly across the row.

Row 16   Work the half tr row with 6 increases evenly across the row.

Row 17   Work the loop st row with 1 increase in the centre space.

Row 18   Work the half tr row, only working along the row with 4 spaces of 1 ch, 1 half tr into the next st, and then make 1 ch sp. Cast off.

To work the ties

Run the yarn through each side edge in turn, using a bodkin, pick up each loop row and into the end of the space row. Pull up to measure 7.5 cm (3 in).

Row 1   Join on and work a half tr row of 8 spaces.

Row 2   Turn with 6 ch, and then work 1½ loop sts into each space across the row.

Row 3   Work the half tr row with 8 spaces.

Row 4   Work as Row 2, but making 2 loop sts into the centre two spaces instead of the 1½ spaces.

Row 5   Repeat Row 3.

Row 6   Repeat Row 4.

Row 7   Work a half tr row making 10 spaces.

Row 8   Work 1½ loop sts into each space across the row.

Row 9   Work a half tr row with 17 spaces.

Row 10   Repeat Row 8. Cast off.

Repeat these 10 rows on the other side.

Border

Work spaces around the unworked edges by making 6 ch, miss 3 loop sts and 1 dc between next two loop sts. Repeat all around the cape including the neck. On the second row work a shell of 9 long treble with a dc between each shell.

A shawl worked in a flower design

Make 240 ch.

Row 1   1 dc into the 10th ch from hook, 5 ch, miss 4 ch, 1 dc into the next ch, 3 ch, miss 4 ch, * into the next ch work 1 single loop stitch (pulling up from the back once, 2 ch) 8 times, 4 ch, miss 4 ch, 1 dc into next ch, 5 ch, miss 4 ch, 1 dc into next ch, 5 ch, miss 4 ch, 1 dc into next ch, 5 ch, miss 4 ch, 1 dc into next ch, 3 ch, miss 4 ch, and repeat from * along row to end. Turn with 10 chain.

Row 2   1 dc into centre ch of first loop ch; 5 ch, 1 dc into next loop, 3 ch * into space between first 2 loop stitches work triple loop stitch (pull up 3 strands) 4 ch. Working between each pair of loop stitches make a triple loop as before and 4 ch between each (7 petals) 3 ch, 1 dc into the next loop ch, (5 ch, 1 dc into next ch) twice, 3 ch, miss next dc, then repeat from * along row, ending with last flower, 3 ch, 1 dc into next loop, 5 ch, 1 dc into next loop, 5 ch, 1 dc into turning ch. Turn with 10 chain.

Row 3   Join on lurex into loop before 3 ch before beginning of flower, 5 ch, 1 dc into space between each pair of petals, * 4 ch, miss 3 ch space and 1 dc; into the following centre double crochet work a loop stitch of 6 strands, 4 ch, 1 dc into space between first

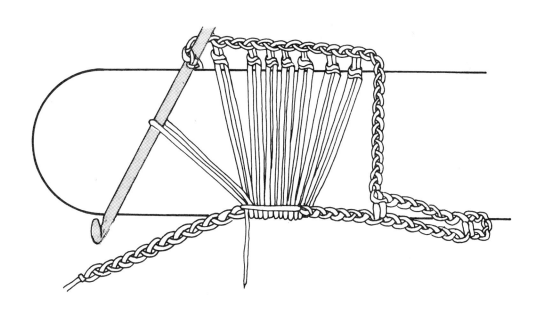

Diagram 48   Commencing the petal and bud pattern

41

two petals of flower of previous row, repeat between each pair of flowers; repeat from * along row ending with 1 dc into loop after last flower. Break off lurex.

Row 4   Join wool at first lurex loop with 1 dc, 5 ch. Work over flower and bud in this way along row, (5 ch, 1 dc over flower, 4 ch, 1 dc into top of bud, 4 ch) 5 times.

Row 5   Join on 3rd 5 ch loop from bud, with 1 dc (over 3rd petal) 3 ch, make row of flowers and buds as previous rows (7) ending with 3 ch, 1 dc into next ch, (5 ch, 1 dc into next ch) twice *(figure 22)*.

Petal and bud

Make 48 ch.

Row 1   1 dc into the 10th chain from the hook, 5 chain, miss 4 chain, 1 dc into the next chain, 3 ch, miss 4 ch, * into the next chain work 1 single loop stitch (pulling up from the back 2 ch) 8 times, 1 ch, miss 4 ch, 1 dc into the next stitch, 5 ch, miss 4 ch, 1 dc into the next ch, 5 ch, miss 4 ch, 1 dc into the next ch, 5 ch, miss 4 ch, 1 dc into the next ch, 3 ch miss 4 ch, and repeat from * along to the end of the row. Turn with 10 chain *(figure 23 and diagrams 48 & 49)*.

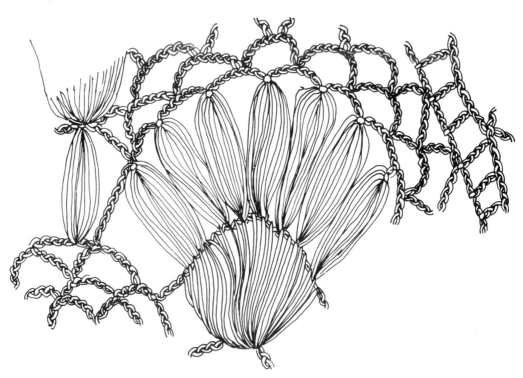

Diagram 49   Working the petal and bud pattern

5 FILET CROCHET

Historical background

The appeal of filet crochet has been its simplicity and the quickness of working it. It consists of the reproduction of any design which is worked on a squared ground such as with filet lace, or tapestry and cross stitch. When drawn on squared paper, the design is very easily followed.

Filet crochet became popular at the beginning of the nineteeth century when lace-trimmed bed linen and table-cloths became fashionable. It was of a heavier thread than that used for the making of lace, but was more durable for frequent use. Unfortunately, this was another craft to be laid aside during the two World Wars, but for the last twenty years interest has again been stimulated in the making of lace and crochet *(figure 24)*.

Italian designers were among the first to recognise the potential for using the filet crochet for fashion and the styles which they created have been copied and improved upon in Europe and in the USA.

The basic method

Filet crochet is composed of solid and open squares. The white square in the design stands for an open square and a square filled in with black lines stands for a solid square.

The work is done in horizontal rows, turning at the end of each row and the diagram must be followed alternately from right to left and once from left to right.

A row of chain forms the foundation row and to assess the chain one counts 3 chain for each square, open or solid.

If a row begins with a solid square add 4 ch extra; if by an open square, add 6 ch.

To begin the row with a solid square

Make the required chain.

Turn, miss 4 ch, and work 1 tr into each of the next 3 ch (this will form together with the turning chain, 4 tr in the first square).

To continue with open squares, work * 2 ch, miss 2 ch, 1 tr into the 3rd stitch, repeat from * *(diagram 50)*.

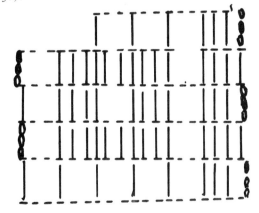

Diagram 50   Working open and solid squares

To begin the first row with an open square

Miss 8 sts of the chain after turning and work 1 tr into the ninth st, which gives the first open square.

Fig. 24   A corner of filet crochet

Continue by working * 2 ch, miss 2 sts of the ch, 1 tr into the third st; repeat from *.

If the next row begins without increase or decrease

With an open square, work 5 ch, at the end of the previous row, turn. In the following row, work 1 tr into the second tr of the previous row, to form the first open square, * 2 ch, miss the 2 ch, 1 tr into the next tr, repeat from * and make the necessary number of squares.

If the next row begins without increase or decrease

With a solid square work 3 ch at the end of the previous row, turn, miss the first tr, work 1 tr into each of the next 3 tr; the 3 ch at the beginning counting as 1 tr; we thus have a solid square of 4 tr.

To work several solid squares in succession

Remember that the first solid square consists of 4 tr (including the last tr of the preceeding open square), and that the solid squares that follow require only 3 tr each. Thus a solid square counts 4 tr; 2 solid squares in succession 7 tr; 3 solid sq. 10 tr; 4 sol sq. 13 tr.

To work a decrease by an open square at the end of the row

Do not work the last open square; 5 ch, turn, 1 tr into the second tr of the previous row, continue the pattern (diagram 51).

To work a decrease by an open square at the beginning of a row

Work as far as the last square shown, 1 ch, turn. 4 ss

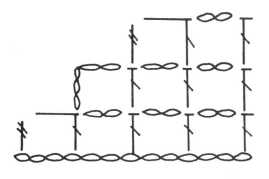

Diagram 51 Working a decrease by an open square at the end of a row

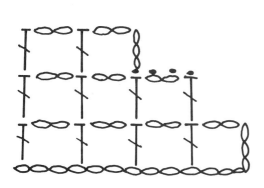
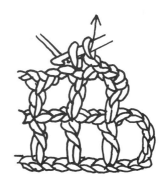

Diagram 52 Working a decrease by an open square at the beginning of a row

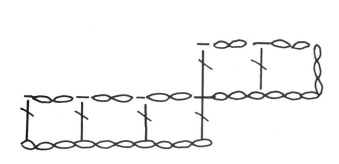
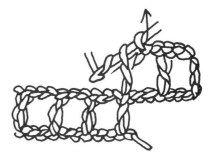

Diagram 53 To increase by an open square at the beginning of a row

into the sts of the last open square, 5 ch, 1 tr into the next tr; continue in pattern *(diagram 52)*.

To increase by an open square at the beginning of a row

Work 8 ch, turn, 1 tr into the first tr (the one which preceeds the 8 ch), 2 ch, 1 tr into the next tr, continue the pattern *(diagram 53)*.

To increase by an open square at the end of the row

Work 5 ch, 1 tr into the stitch which already contains the last tr (the one which preceeds the 5 ch), 1 ch, turn, 3 ss into the first ch; then in order to increase at the beginning of the next row, 8 ch, 1 tr into the st already containing the last ss *(diagram 54)*.

To decrease by a solid square at the end of a row

Work along the row, leaving unworked the last square, turn, ss along the top of the first two trebles, 3 ch, 1 tr into each of the next 2 ch, 1 tr into the next tr, and continue with the pattern *(diagram 55)*.

To decrease by a solid square at the beginning of a row

Work as far as the last square, 3 ch, turn, 1 tr into each of the next 2 ch and 1 tr into the next tr. Continue with the pattern *(diagram 56)*.

To increase by a solid square at the end of a row

Work along the row to the last tr, 1 tr into the base of this last tr, and repeat for the required number of squares *(diagram 57)*.

To increase by a solid square at the beginning of a row

Work along the row, make 9 tr, and work 1 tr into each of the next 5 ch, and 1 tr into the next tr *(diagram 58)*.

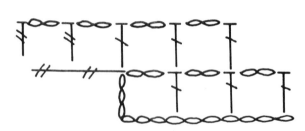

Diagram 54   To increase by an open square at the end of a row

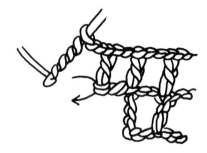

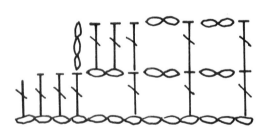

Diagram 55   To decrease by a solid square at the end of a row

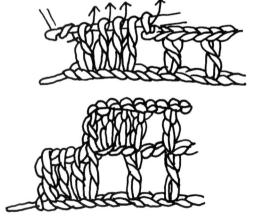

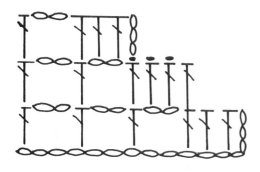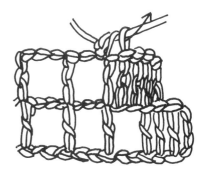

Diagram 56   To decrease by a solid square at the beginning of a row

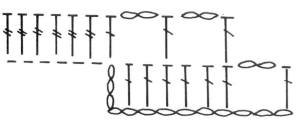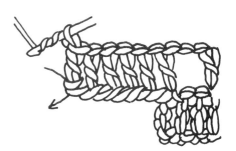

Diagram 57   To increase by a solid square at the end of a row

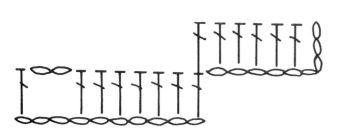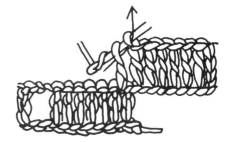

Diagram 58   To increase by a solid square at the beginning of a row

6 FRAMEWOVEN CROCHET LACE

Historical background

Framewoven lace has its origins in the ancient art of weaving, which over the centuries progressed to a very sophisticated form, initially in China. A simple form reappeared in France early in the nineteenth century and was recognised as a folk craft. Framewoven lace was introduced into Spain and Portugal following the two World Wars and is currently in great demand by tourists. It requires little concentration for many of the attractive results and can be attempted by young and old.

Improvising and assembling a frame

To improvise the frame

Inside measurements   19.3 cm (7½ in), square
Outside   23.6 cm (9¼ in), square
Width of wood   2.5 cm (1 in)
Depth of wood   1.3 cm (½ in)
Pin nails 2.5 cm (1 in), 13 on each side placed at 2 cm (¾ in) intervals
A ball of yarn
A bodkin

To assemble the frame

Screw the four sides together and rub smooth with sandpaper and prepare for the pin nails. Pencil a line for inserting pins at 2 cm (¾ in) intervals and 1.3 cm (½ in) above surface. There should be 13 nails on each side of small frame *(diagram 59)*.

Basic method

Winding the frame

Start with the third pin nail on side 1 of the frame. Tie the yarn securely and take across the frame, pass it around the third nail on side 3 opposite and back again. Move on to the next and fourth nail side 1, repeat until two nails are left on the side of the frame. Carry thread on the outside of the frame to the third nail on side 2 and wind across the frame to the third nail, side 4. This will give threads at right angles to the first set *(diagrams 60 & 61)*.

The winding is now carried out twice more, but diagonally, starting at the fifth nail and work across to the fifth nail round the corner *(diagrams 62 & 63)*.

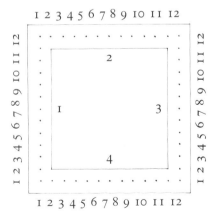

Diagram 59   Assembling the frame and spacing the pins

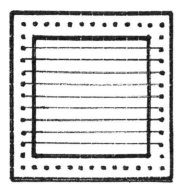

Diagram 60   Laying the first threads horizontally

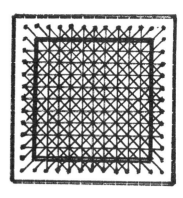

Diagram 63   Laying the last threads diagonally

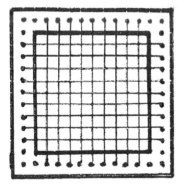

Diagram 61   Laying the second threads vertically

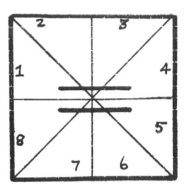

Diagram 64   To knot vertically

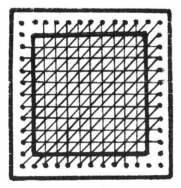

Diagram 62   Laying the third threads diagonally

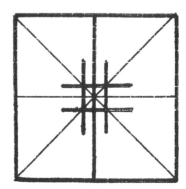

Diagram 65   To complete the knotting

50

To work the knotting

Take a length of thread on a large needle or shuttle.

Each part where the four sets of threads cross must be tightly knotted with four knots, 2 vertically, 2 horizontally.

Bring thread from back up in space 1, and take down through space 4. Twist the thread around the needle underneath the work to hold before bringing through the front again. Bring needle up in space 8 and down through space 5. Repeat this up in space 2 and down through space 7; then up in space 3 and down through space 6. Carry the thread along and repeat on each square for the pattern *(diagrams 64 & 65)*.

To complete the work

To remove the work from the frame use a sharp blade, cutting the threads as close to the nails as possible. Lay the work flat and comb out the fringe and trim with scissors.

The fringes can be either brushed to make them fluffy, or can be left straight *(figure 25)*.

Larger articles are worked in squares and either sewn or crocheted together when finished.

To make an edging

Twist the yarn over the front of one pin and then around the back of the next pin. Carry it along the edge of the frame and back again putting it inside on the 2nd row where it was outside in the 1st row. Make a buttonhole stitch at every pin, covering all the yarn at that point.

Fig. 25   Completed mat

To make a shawl

This would be made in the same way as the small mat.

The frame takes the measurements of the size of the shawl and is assembled in the same way as for the mat. The knotting is worked as before.

Before removing from the frame, layer four threads around the perimeter. Then proceed to work the edging as given in the previous paragraph.

Neaten all ends and add a fringe to the two shorter sides, after removing from the frame *(figures 26 & 27)*.

A variation of the knotting is shown in figure 28 and in diagrams 66 & 67.

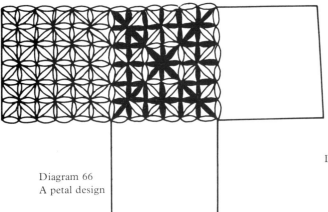

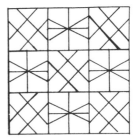

Diagram 67   A design of squares and crosses

Diagram 66
A petal design

Fig. 26   Petal design detail

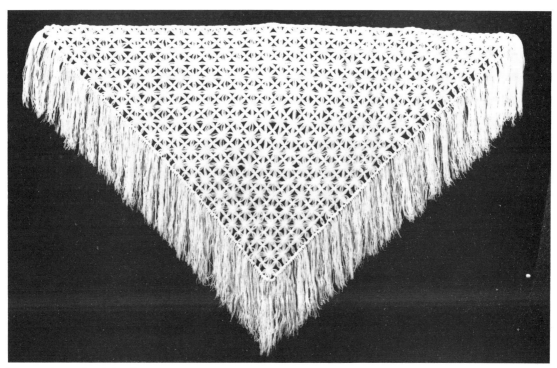

Fig. 27   A completed shawl

Fig. 28   Detail of a variation

7 HAIRPIN LACE CROCHET

Historical background

It is not possible to date hairpin lace crochet lace definitely, which is rather surprising considering its difference from other techniques. The finished work certainly has taken lace for its inspiration, but the choice of the tool has remained obscure.

In old French patterns the tool was made of wood and resembled a fork, hence its name *la fourche*, and the patterns possibly dated from the early nineteenth century. There was a distant resemblance to an earlier tool, which was called a lucet and was used for the making of braids. In the years between 1800 and 1900 it was quite common to use ordinary hairpins to make these braids, but machine made laces soon took

Fig. 29   Tools and materials. *From left to right; back row:* crochet cotton, embroidery silk, double knitting yarn, lurex, synthetic yarn and string; *centre row:* Hairpin frame 6.25 cm (2½ in), raffia; *front row:* crochet hooks, scissors, safety pins, darning needle, rubber bands and small hairpin prong

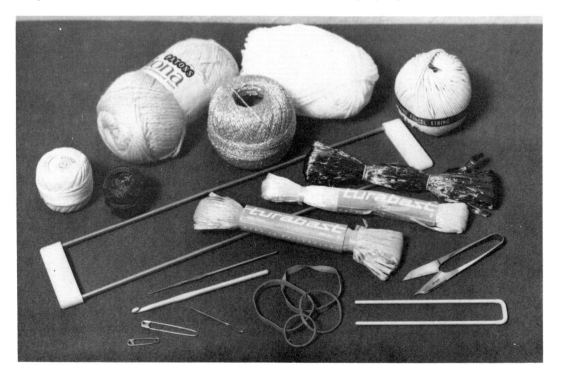

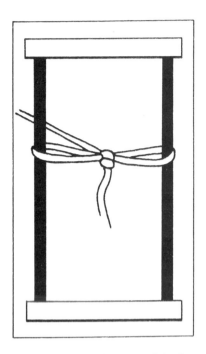
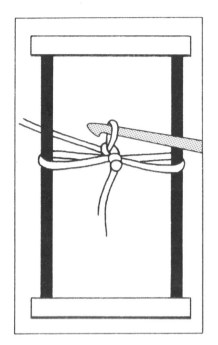

Diagram 68   Attaching the loop around the frame and
tying at the centre

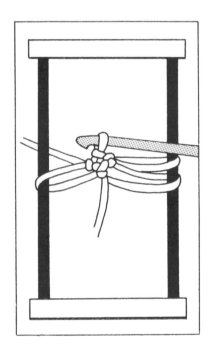

Diagrams 69 & 70   Inserting the hook through the front
of the left loop and completing a double crochet

the place of these edgings and it was not until the middle of the twentieth century that interest revived. With the new use of crochet for fashion, the character of the fork changed and it is now a larger adjustable version of the old hairpin.

The Mediterranean countries soon adapted to the fashions and visitors to these countries carried samples of the craft back to their own homes. There has been a great appreciation in the USA, where exhibitions have shown varied and considerable interest in hairpin crochet, and it is being encouraged in the UK, where the tendency is towards delicate lacelike patterns, with more variety in the stitches.

Tools and materials

The hairpin frame

Hairpin lace is always made on a frame, the width of which is dictated by the chosen project and the stitch being worked with a crochet hook.

It is possible to buy the larger frame in any wool shop or in the wool department of the larger stores. These are manufactured in widths ranging from 6 mm ($\frac{1}{4}$ in) up to 6.5 cm ($2\frac{1}{2}$ in). To obtain widths larger than this, it would be advisable to make one's own bar. This is described below.

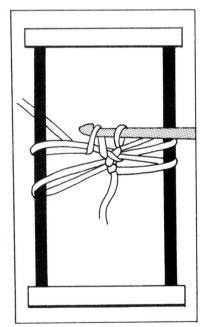

Diagram 71 Turn the frame and complete another double crochet

Improvising a frame

If a frame has been difficult to obtain, two number 7 knitting needles and some dowelling are a good substitute.

1. Take off the knob from the end of each needle.
2. Cut off the points with a hacksaw.
3. Smooth off with a file.

To make the wooden bars

1. Choose wood dowel 13 mm ($\frac{1}{2}$ in) in diameter.
2. Cut dowel to 10 cm (4 in) in length.
3. Drill two holes the same size as the needles to make a tight fit. These holes must not be drilled right through the dowel, but to a sufficient depth to make the needle rigid and there must be 7.5 cm (3 in) between the holes.
4. Place the bars on each end of the uprights and secure with rubber bands.

Materials suitable for Hairpin crochet

Yarn, wool, lurex, cotton, raffia and string (figure 29).

The two basic methods

To work method 1

1. Tie the yarn tightly round the frame in a double knot.
2. Take the free end of the yarn over the loop at the centre.
3. Tie another double knot at the centre to divide the large loop into two smaller loops (diagram 68).
4. Take the working end of the yarn from the front of the frame round the right-hand side to the back and hold the yarn in the left hand.
5. With the crochet hook in the right hand, place the hook through the loop on the left-hand side of the frame (diagram 69)
6. Draw the yarn through the loop.
7. Take the hook over the loop and pick up the yarn (diagram 69).
8. Draw the yarn through the one loop already on the hook (diagram 70).
9. Continue to hold the yarn in the left hand, push the crochet hook backwards through the frame and turn the frame to the left.
10. Place the hook under the top loop on the left side of the frame and draw the yarn through (diagram 71).

To work method 2

Take the bar off the frame and with the yarn make a loop. Slip this on the right upright of the frame *(diagram 72)*.

Pull the knot of the loop to the centre of the frame with the yarn at the back. Hold the frame in the left hand and with the right hand turn the frame a half turn to the left *(diagrams 73 & 74)*. Insert the hook into the front of the loop, which is now on the left-hand side, catch the yarn and pull this through the loop, put the yarn over the hook and pull this through the loop to complete a double crochet *(diagram 75)*.

The crochet hook is now held horizontally across the frame and with the right hand take the shaft of the hook through to the back of the frame before turning the latter a half turn to the left as before *(diagrams 76 & 77)*. Insert the hook under the front of the left-hand loop, catch the yarn over the hook, pull it through the loop and complete the double crochet *(diagrams 78 & 79)*.

The stitch should at all times be controlled between the thumb and the first finger of the left hand in order that it remains in the centre of the frame.

Complete the required number of loops, having checked this on both uprights. An aid to this is to mark every 50 loops, whilst working, with a coloured thread.

To complete the strip

After the last loop has been worked, cut, and leave an end 10 cm (4 in) long. Pull the end through the last loop and turn the work to the wrong side. The end is threaded through the eye of a blunt darning needle and it is then taken through each diagonal stitch of the spine.

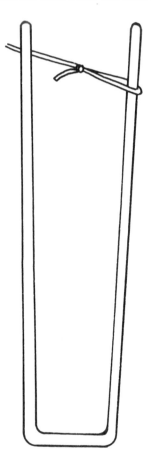

Diagram 72   Slipping the loop on to the upright for method 2

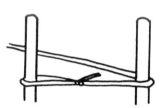

Diagram 73   Pulling the knot to the front centre of the frame

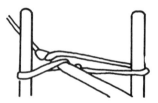

Diagram 74   Turning the frame a half turn to the left

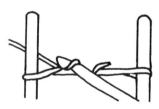

Diagram 75   Working a double crochet in the loop

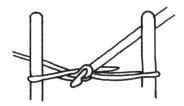 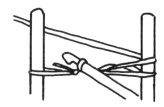

Diagrams 76 & 77   Taking the hook to the back of the frame and turning as before

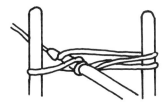 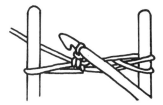

Diagrams 78 & 79   Completing a double crochet in left hand loop

The lower bar is now removed and the strip carefully slipped from the frame.

Whilst working the strip it may be found that the number of loops become too crowded. The best way to deal with this is to slip the majority of the loops from the frame, having first of all taken off the lower bar. A manageable number of loops left on the frame is about twenty, and the remainder of the strip is carefully folded up and secured with an elastic band. Replace the bar and complete the strip.

To work the stitches for the spine

Double crochet into the front of a loop

For this stitch follow the basic method.

Double crochet under the whole of a loop

Wind the yarn around the frame as previously explained, and, with the yarn, tie in the centre to make the two starting loops. Turn the frame one half turn and make a double crochet into the left-hand loop. Turn the frame as before, but this time insert the hook under the whole loop of the left-hand side before making the double crochet *(figures 30 & 31)*.

Work up the frame in this way working under the whole loop instead of through the loop on the left-hand side. Complete the strip as before.

Treble stitch in front of a loop

This is worked in the same manner as for the double crochet of the basic method. Form the two starting loops as explained, followed by the half turn of the frame, but instead of making a double crochet into the front of the left-hand loop, put the yarn over the hook before inserting it into the loop, put the yarn again over the hook and take off the loops two at a time. Continue to turn the frame and make a treble stitch into the loop for the necessary number of loops. Finish and neaten the strip as previously explained.

Double crochet and treble stitches under the same loop

This method is worked as before, but the double crochet and the treble stitch are both placed into the same left-hand loop. Continue to work up the frame for the required number of loops and fasten off.

A puff stitch under the whole loop

This stitch is described in basic crochet stitches, and can be used in the place of either the double crochet or treble stitches. As this is a more bulky stitch, the use of the whole loop is necessary, so, instead of inserting the crochet hook under the front of the loop, put the hook under the whole loop on the left hand side.

59

Fig. 30   A car rug, working under the whole loop

Fig. 31 Details of the car rug

A block of 3 trebles into the loop

In the place of working a double crochet into each loop, a solid spine is made by using 3 trebles into each left-hand loop. However, this would require a careful choice of yarn to avoid a crowded design.

Bar stitch into the left hand loop

Work a double crochet under a complete loop, followed by 4 chain stitches. This will form a bar and gives an open pattern to the spine *(diagram 80)*.

Strip grouping

Fan edging

Divide the number of loops into equal groups; for example, using for the pattern worked on a 7.5 cm (3 in) frame a multiple of 30 loops.

This would give a width of 7.5 cm (3 in) for the pattern, which would be repeated along the row over these 30 loops.

To work the fan upper edge

Complete the required number of loops on the frame, slip them carefully off the prongs and neaten the ends as previously explained.

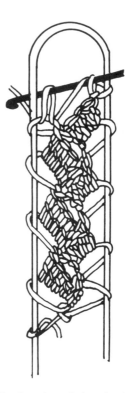

Diagram 80   Putting a bar stitch under the loop

61

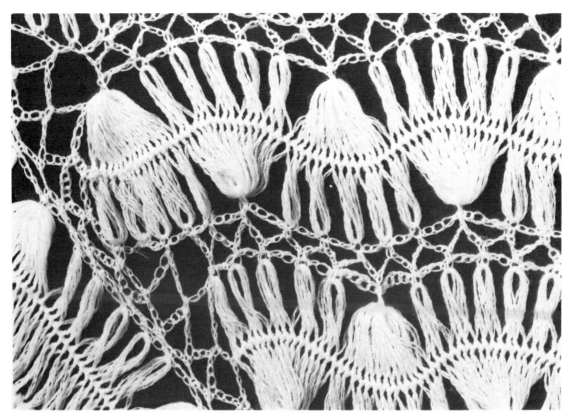

Fig. 32 Working a fan group

Place the strip horizontally on a flat surface and with a fresh ball of yarn join into the first loop of the top right corner. Insert the hook into this loop and take up the following next two loops, the hook pointing in from the back of the strip through to the front *(figure 32)*. This will form a figure eight. Pull the yarn through and complete a double crochet. Work 3 chain, and repeat from * 4 times more, but end the last repeat with 5 chain instead of 3 chain. Continue along the row by inserting the hook through the next 15 loops and, holding them together under the thumb, make a double crochet in the whole group. This group must be untwisted, so the hook goes in from the front to the back. Finish with 5 chain * and repeat from * to * along the strip.

Working the lower edge

Reverse the strip having the lower edge now at the top.

Starting at the top right-hand loop commence with 1 double crochet into the first 15 loops, still un-

twisted, 5 chain, then twist 5 more groups of three with 3 chain between each group, but finishing with 5 chain instead of 3 chain in the last repeat.

Each strip is worked in this way to the end and the strip are now ready for joining *(diagram 81)*.

A fan design shawl

Begin by working a number of strips containing the following loops: 255, 225, 195, 165, 135, 105 and 75.

Place each strip in its correct order, one above the other. Join each pair of strips with a zigzag chain.

Care must be taken that the same number of loops are left free at the beginning and the end of the joining of any two strips *(figure 33)*. Commence with the two largest strips and place the 255 loops above the 225 strip.

Join the yarn in the 3rd set of loops of the top strip, working from right to left. Work 1 dc into the join, make 3 ch, 1 dc into the first set of loops of the 2nd strip, 3 ch, 1 dc into the next set of loops of the top strip. Repeat this zigzag chain using every set of loops

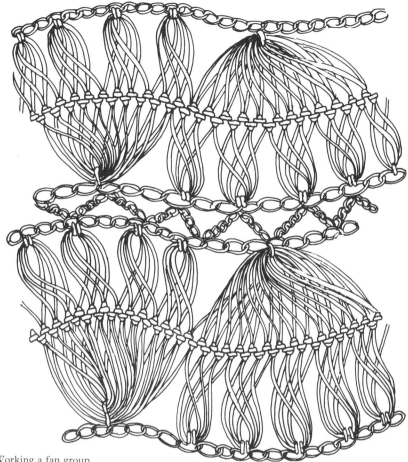

Diagram 81   Working a fan group

along the row. This should end by leaving two sets of loops unworked at the end of the row.

The remaining rows are joined in the same manner.

To work the edging

Join a new length of yarn into the top right-hand stitch and work 1 dc into the same join. Continue working down the right edge towards the bottom of the shawl by making 7 ch and 1 dc into the next spine centre. Work loosely, continuing in this way around the three sides of the shawl, filling in the gaps between the strips.

When reaching the bottom edge allow for the curve there by making more chain where required, so that the pattern is not distorted.

Turn the work at the top left hand corner and repeat the row of loop chains working into the loops and not into the chain itself. When these two rows have been completed, crochet two rows of treble loosely along the top edge and fasten off.

Add a fringe around the three edges by cutting lengths of yarn 45 cm (18 in) and, with the hook, knot them into each chain loop.

Bud grouping

On the frame work a number of loops to a multiple of 3, preferably working into the front of each loop. Take the strip off the frame and neaten the ends.

Upper edge

Lay the strip on a flat surface and join on a new ball of yarn into the top right-hand loop. Insert the hook in this first loop from the back to the front of the work and repeat this into the following two loops. Holding all three loops between the thumb and the forefinger, work a double crochet into the group.

The group is now twisted, and this is now followed by 3 chain. Repeat the group and 3 chain along the row.

63

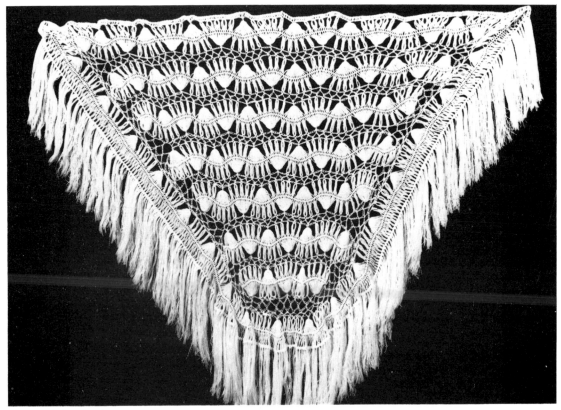

Fig. 33   A fan shawl

Fig. 34   A bud group design

Lower edge

Reverse the work and commence by making a join into the top right-hand loop as on the previous edge.

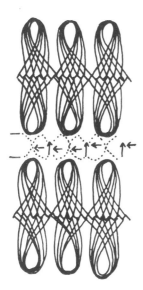

Diagram 82   Bud grouping

The pattern is repeated as before, and each bud should pair with the bud of the opposite edge (diagram 82 and figure 34).

Working a strip into a circle

Make a strip of 48 loops, which is a practical working number for a circle, fasten off the yarn and slip the end through the diagonal stitches on the wrong side of the work. Cut the surplus end.

Thread a large-eyed darning needle with a length of buttonhole thread roughly 15 cm (6 in) long. Take up each loop from front to back and do not twist. The effect is neater if the taking up is started in the middle of the row and not at either end. Pull up the loops and tie securely with a reef knot, i.e. the left thread over the right thread and tie, repeat right thread over the left. This brings the strip of loops into a circle. Thread a needle with some yarn or thread and on the wrong side of the strip draw each side of the spine together and secure with a second stitch (diagram 83).

Neaten edges and the outer edge is now ready for working the chosen edge grouping.

A stole using small circles

Materials
8 balls of 2 ply baby yarn
An Aero hairpin frame 4.5 cm (1¾ in)
Crochet hooks 2.50 and 4.00
A bodkin and a darning needle
Buttonhole thread to match yarn

This would work a stole measuring 150 cm (60 in) in length and 50 cm (20 in) in width.

To work the small motifs

Begin the work by using the 2 ply yarn singly and with the basic method. This will make an open and lacey effect. Continue working up the frame by making 48 loops on each upright. Leave an end about 5 cm (2 in) long, cut the yarn and pass the end through the last loop. Thread the bodkin with a length of buttonhole thread and, having slipped the strip from the frame, thread the cotton through each loop. A neater effect is achieved if starting at a loop in the middle of the strip and, after having reached the last loop, the remainder of the loops at the beginning are then taken up, meeting once again those in the middle (diagram 84). Pull the thread into a tight circle and tie with a double knot. Neaten all ends by slipping them back through the spine. Again using the buttonhole thread, join the two ends of the spine together and neaten ends, tying firmly as before.

Make the necessary number of motifs – 15, 13, 15, 13, 15 and 8 half motifs.

To join the first row of motifs

The first motif is completed by using a 4.00 hook and working 1 dc into any pair of loops (T). Keeping the chain easy make 4 ch, 1 dc into the next pair of loops (T) all round the edge, ending with 4 ch, and join into the first dc with a ss.

Joining the second and the first motifs together

On the first motif work * 4 ch, 1 ss into the centre stitch of the next chain-loop and repeat from * 7 times more; work 2 ch, work 1 ss into the centre of any chain-loop of a second motif, 2 ch, 1 ss into the centre of the next loop of the first motif (figure 35).

Repeat this joining three times more and complete the second motif by working all round the edge with 4

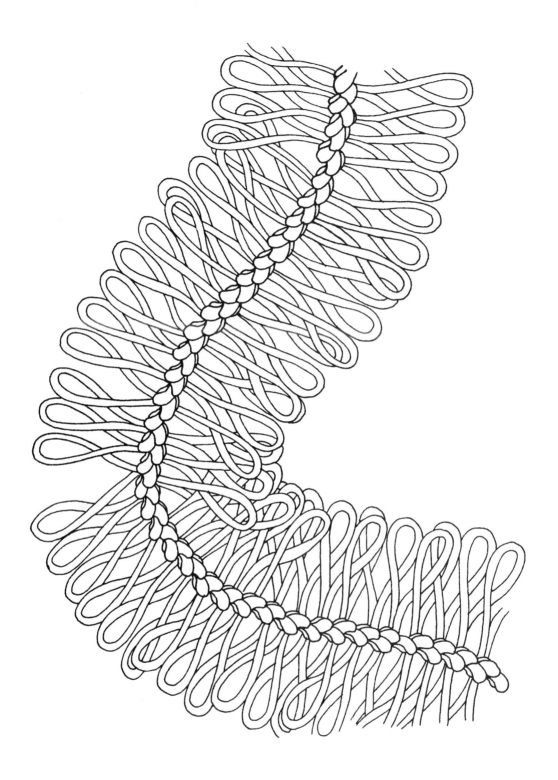

Diagram 83   Taking the strip off the frame

ch, 1 ss into the centre stitch of the next chain-loop. Continue to join each pair of motifs in this way along the row until 15 motifs have been joined together horizontally.

Start to join the motifs from the right-hand side of the work and complete the second row motif with a chain-loop row and ending with a ss to join the circle. Place the motif beneath and between the first and second motifs of the top row (diagram 85). * Work 2 ch, ss into the centre stitch of the 4th chain-loop counting from the join of the first and second motif of the top row (figure 36); 2 ch, ss into the centre stitch of a 4 chain-loop on the second row motif; 2 ch, ss into the next free chain-loop on the first upper motif, 2 ch, ss into the next free chain-loop on the lower motif. Repeat this until there are 4 joins, ending with 2 ch, ss into the next free loop on the lower motif; 2 ch, 1 ss into the next free loop on the second upper motif, 2 ch, ss into the next free loop on the first lower motif, 2 ch, and repeat for 4 joins, 2 ch, ss into next free loop on the lower motif; 4 ch, ss into the next loop, repeat from * all round, end with ss to first dc to join. Break off yarn.

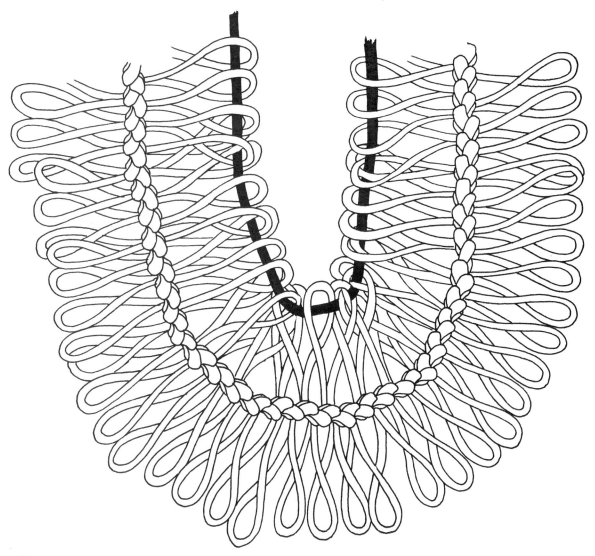

Diagram 84   Threading the loops and joining the strip into a circle

Take another motif and repeat the joining

Work the first row of chain-loops on the second motif ending with a ss to join the circle, 2 ch, ss into the centre of the fourth chain-loop from the last join in the top row. Repeat the zigzag chain into the following 4 chain-loops; 2 ch, ss into the centre of the next free chain-loop of the second motif in the top row. Make 4 joins of zigzag chain in the next following pairs of free chain-loops. Join in this way the next 4 free chain-loops of third motif in the top row to the second motif in the second row.

All the motifs are joined together in this way. The spaces are filled with half motifs *(figure 37)*.

A shawl using large circles

Materials
Mohair yarn 9 × 20 g (6 oz) balls
Yarn to match 4 × 25 g ($3\frac{1}{2}$ oz) balls
1 reel buttonhole thread to match
Hairpin frame 7.5 cm (3 in)

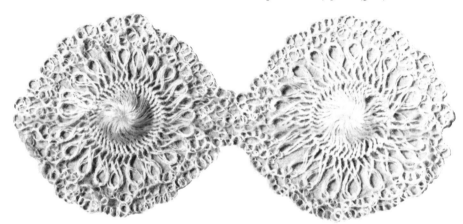

Fig. 35   Joining the first and second motifs of the first row

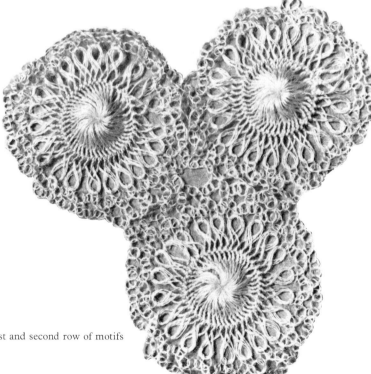

Fig. 36   Joining the first and second row of motifs

68

Aero hairpin frame 4.5 cm ($1\frac{3}{4}$ in)
Crochet hooks 3.50 and 2.50
Measurements
Shawl 152 cm (60 in) × 91 cm (36 in) excluding the
    fringe
Motif 15.5 cm (6 in) diameter
Number of motifs in each row: 10, 9, 8, 7, 6, 5 and 9
    half motifs for spaces *(figure 38)*

Diagram 85   Position of motif in the second row

Working the motifs

The previous instructions for making the small circles are followed, but in this example a 7.5 cm (3 in) hairpin frame is used instead of the 4.5 cm ($1\frac{3}{4}$ in) together with the 3.50 hook.

Knot stitch edge

The hairpin circle has been completed and the outer edge ready for working. This is done by taking a blunt darning needle and a fine yarn to match the main motif.

Starting at the right and 13 mm ($\frac{1}{2}$ in) inside the outside edge, work (from right to left) a knot stitch over each pair of loops *(diagrams 86 & 87 and figure 39)*.

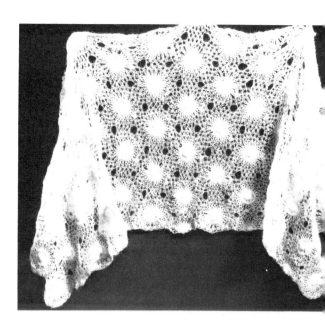

Fig. 37   A hairpin stole with small circle motifs

Fig. 38   A hairpin shawl with large circles

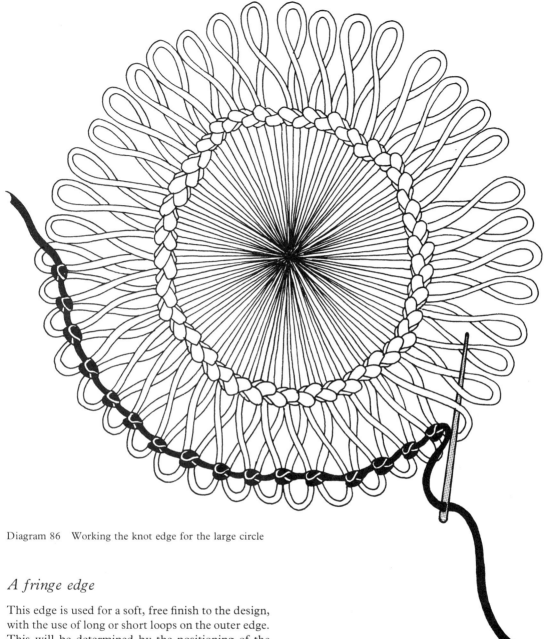

Diagram 86   Working the knot edge for the large circle

A fringe edge

This edge is used for a soft, free finish to the design, with the use of long or short loops on the outer edge. This will be determined by the positioning of the spine, which can be either in the middle between the prongs or nearer to one prong than the other.

Working the inner edge

Join the yarn on to the frame by making a loop and slipping this on the right-hand prong as previously explained.

Continue to make the required number of loops,

i.e. a multiple of 10. * Work 1 dc into the first 10 loops (u), 5 ch, repeat from * all around the edge. Leave the outer edge unworked.

An alternative fringe edge

Join on as previously explained, but after slipping the loop on the right-hand prong, pull the knot of the

71

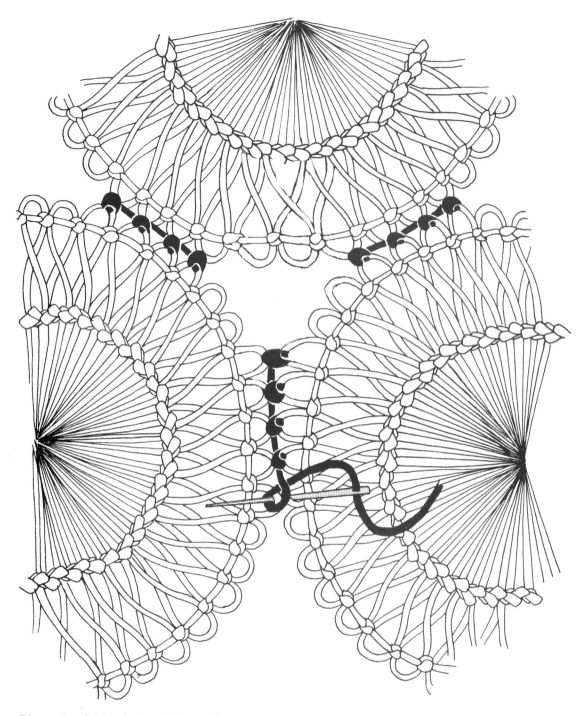

Diagram 87   Joining the large circles together

loop to about 12.5 mm ($\frac{1}{2}$ in) away from this prong.

Continue to work the number of loops required, but taking care to hold the spine firmly between the thumb and first finger of the left hand. This will ensure that the spine stitches will be kept in a straight line *(diagram 88)*. Finish the strip and neaten the ends.

This method will form an effective base for a braid,

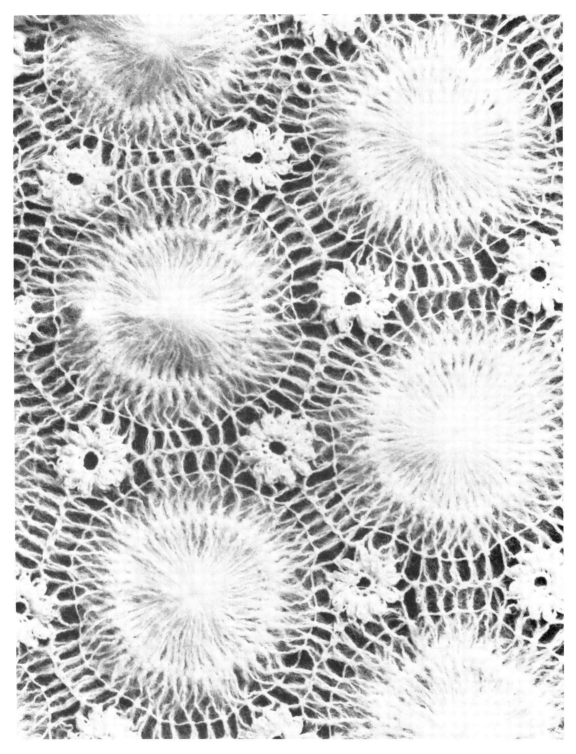

Fig. 39   Detail of circles

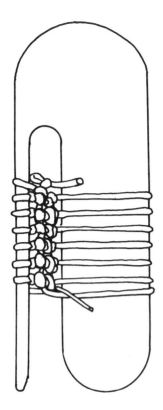

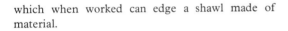

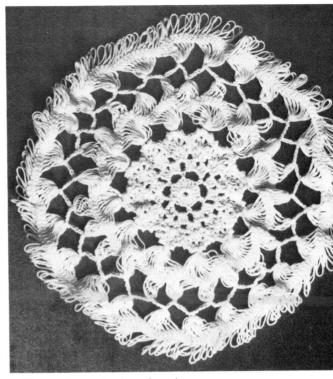

Diagram 88   An early hairpin prong used for fringing

Fig. 40   A mat showing a free edge

which when worked can edge a shawl made of material.

A Turkish mat design

Hairpin crochet lace used in conjunction with crochet.

To make the centre motif

Commence with 6 ch and join with a ss into the first ch to make a ring.

Round 1   Work 18 tr into the ring and join with a ss into the top of the first treble.

Round 2   1 dc into the same place as the last join, * 6 ch, miss 2 tr, 1 dc into the next tr and repeat from * all round, ss to the first dc (6 spaces).

Round 3   Ss into the first space, 3 ch, 2 tr into the same sp, 2 ch, 3 tr into the same sp (1 shell made). * 2 ch, miss 1 dc and into the next sp work 3 tr, 2 ch, 3 tr. Repeat from * ending with 2 ch, ss into the top of the first 3 ch.

Round 4   Ss across the first 3 tr and into the 2 ch sp, 3 ch, 1 tr into the same sp, 2 ch, 2 tr into the same sp. *Work 3 tr, 2 ch, 3 tr into the next sp and repeat from * all round and join with ss into the top of the first 3 ch (12 groups).

Round 5   Ss across the first 2 tr and into the ch sp, 5 ch; into the next 2 ch sp work (1 long tr, 1 ch) 4 times, 1 dc into the next sp between the shell groups, * 1 ch, into next 2 ch sp work (1 long tr, 1 ch) 5 times, 1 dc into the space between the shell groups. Repeat from * all round.

To work the first hairpin strip

Make a strip of 180 loops

To join the hairpin strip to the centre motif

Join on yarn to any shell of the centre motif. In the space between the first and second tr make 1 dc, 3 ch, 1 dc. Repeat this picot in the space between the third and fourth tr. Work 1 dc in the 15 loops of the hairpin strip all together, joining this to the centre

74

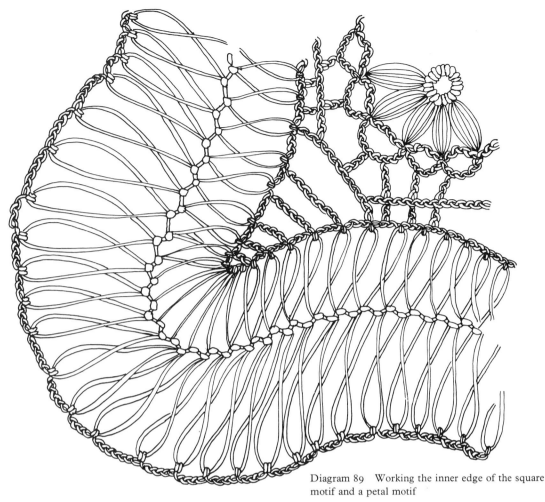

Diagram 89 Working the inner edge of the square motif and a petal motif

motif. Repeat the picots in the remainder of the shell and to the centre of the next shell. Join the next 15 loops of the hairpin strip, making a dc as before and joining it to the centre of the next shell. Repeat this all round (12 groups).

To work a strip into a square

The square is commenced as with all other shapes, by working a strip of loops, in this case 136. Slip these from the frame and neaten all the ends.

To make the second hairpin strip

Make a strip of 240 loops

To work the inner edge

To join the second strip to the first hairpin strip

On the free side of the first strip starting at the join, work 1 dc into 10 loops (T) using the last 5 loops plus the first 5 loops at the join, 5 ch, 1 dc into the next 10 loops (T) of second strip, 5 ch, 1 dc into 5 loops of the first strip; 5 ch 1 dc into 10 loops of the second strip, 5 ch, 1 dc into 10 loops of the first strip, 5 ch, 1 dc into 10 loops of the second strip, 5 ch, 1 dc into 5 loops of the first strip. Repeat this zigzag joining all round. Join with a ss. Leave all the loops on the outside of the second strip unworked *(figure 40)*.

Attach the yarn to the first loop of the strip, starting at the right-hand side and make 1 double crochet into the same loop. ★ (Work 4 ch, 1 dc into the next loop of the strip) 9 times, (1 dc through the next 4 loops) twice (u), 1 dc through the next 4 loops. With a small safety-pin mark the loop on the opposite side of the strip, which will be between the second and the third loops of this 4 loop group, (1 dc through the next 4 loops) twice, and 1 dc in the next loop; 2 ch, turn the work, miss the last 7 dc and ss across into the next 4 ch sp, 2 ch, turn, 1 dc back into the next free loop on the strip, 2 ch, turn, ss into the next 4 ch sp, 2 ch, turn, 1 dc back into the next free loop of the strip, 2 ch, turn, 1 treble into the next 4 ch sp, 2 ch, turn, 1 dc in the next loop of the strip, 2 ch, turn, 1 triple treble in the

75

next 4 ch sp, 2 ch, turn, 1 dc in the next loop of the strip; repeat from * 3 times more, ending the last repeat by working the last dc as a ss into the first dc of the strip *(diagram 89)*.

To work the outer edge

Attach the yarn to any marked loop of the outside edge and work 1 dc into the same loop (T), *(4 ch, 1 dc into the next loop) 7 times, 4 ch, 1 dc through the next 2 loops, 1 dc through the next 4 loops, 1 dc through the next 7 loops, 1 dc through the next 4 loops and 1 dc through the next 2 loops; 2 ch, miss last 5 dc, ss in the next 4 ch sp, 2 ch, 1 dc back into the next loop on the strip, (4 ch, 1 dc in the next loop) 7 times; repeat from * along the edge, starting each time at the next marker and joining the last 4 ch to the first dc *(figure 41)*.

Filling motif

When a large version of this design is worked, i.e. on a 7.5 cm (3 in) frame, where any four squares meet, a filling is required. One suggestion is an eight petal motif.

To work a motif

* Begin by winding a new length of yarn four times around the end of a pencil. Slip this off the pencil and work 16 dc into the ring, which has been formed. Join the last dc to the first dc with a ss and into the same place as this join, work a puff stitch *(diagram 89)*. Next make 4 ch * and repeat from * to * 7 times more and join with a ss.

To work the filling

Place the completed motif within the space to be filled and with a safety pin fasten a petal to a loop opposite to it, starting at a corner loop. Attach the remaining seven petals to the corresponding loops. Make 1 dc into any corner loop on the hairpin side, and then using a zigzag chain work 3 ch, 1 dc into the centre of the chain between the petals of the motifs. Continue with 3 ch, 1 dc into the second loop away from the corner, 3 ch, 1 dc into the top of the next petal, 3 ch, miss 1 loop on the hairpin strip and continue in this way until the remainder of the petals have been joined in. *(figure 42)*.

Joining the strips

With a single loop

Place two strips side by side vertically on a flat surface. Beginning at the lower edge, insert the hook into the loop on the right-hand side of the first strip, then repeat the same movement through the first loop of the left-hand side of the second strip *(diagram 90)*. Pull this last loop down through the first loop. Repeat this again first into the next right side and then into the loop of the second strip. Continue up the strip in a zigzag manner until the last loop is reached. Cut the yarn leaving an end about 10 cm (4 in) long.

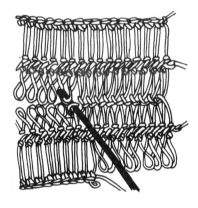

Diagram 90   A single loop join

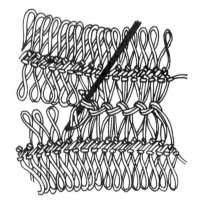

Diagram 91   A double loop join

Fig. 41 A square hairpin motif

Fig. 42 Square motifs joined by chains and small motifs

Double and three loop

The joining is worked in the same way as with a single loop, only this time with either two or three loops at a time. Finish and neaten as previously *(diagram 91)*.

Key pattern

Place two strips side by side vertically with the lower edges level. Begin at the lower edge by inserting the hook into the first 2 loops on the left side and draw the next 2 loops on the same side, down through them; draw through this new loop 2 loops from the right side. Through this loop draw the next 2 loops from the right side. Continue to draw the following 2 loops of the left side through the 2 loops on the right side, twice, and again the step pattern is repeated up the strip using two loops at a time *(diagram 92)*.

Diagram 92   A key pattern join

Zigzag chain

Place two strips together, one above the other horizontally, and work from the right to the left. Using the lower chain edge of the first strip and the upper chain edge of the second strip, make 1 dc into the first stitch of the upper strip *(diagram 93)*.

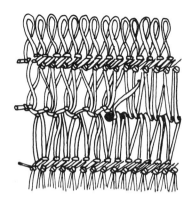

Diagram 93   A zigzag chain

Continue joining together by working 3 ch, 1 dc into the third stitch of the second strip, 3 ch, miss 3 stitches along the lower edge of the first strip and work 1 dc into the next stitch. Make 3 ch and then miss 3 stitches along the upper edge of the second strip and work 1 dc into the next stitch. Continue working in this zigzag manner along the row.

Zigzag pattern with space

Work the chain and double crochet joining as in the previous example, but as the fan pattern will be up the same way for each row, this will leave a space between each fan base along the row. This space can be filled with a flower design as in the shawl pattern given in the next section on surface hairpin crochet.

Insertion joining

This is useful when joining the strips where single loops have been twisted and where it is necessary to break the monotony of a design.

Crochet a row of dc into the twisted loop edges of each strip to be joined. Place two strips one above the other and make a dc in the first dc of either strip, *work 3 ch, miss 1 dc on the corresponding strip and make a dc into the next stitch, 3 ch, miss 1 dc on the first strip and work 1 dc into the next stitch. Repeat this along the row in a zigzag manner.

To join the two strips together, work a dc through the first 5 loops of the free edge of the second strip, 2 ch, and join to the centre st of the first loop of the first strip by dropping the loop from the hook, insert it in the stitch and pull the loop through, * 2 ch, 1 dc in each of the next 3 loops of the second strip, (twist each loop twice), 2 ch, join to the centre stitch of the next loop of the first strip, 2 ch, dc through the next 5 loops of the second strip, keeping the loops straight. Make 2 ch, join to the centre st of the next loop of the first strip, repeat from * across the strip.

Joining with a double slip stitch

Place the strips one above the other and join on the yarn at the right-hand first loop of the lower strip. Insert the hook through the corresponding loop of the top strip and pull the yarn down through the top loop, also through the lower loop of the second strip and then on through the loop st at the commencement. Repeat this along the strip, taking the yarn through the top loop down through the bottom loop of the strip and then through the loop of the ridge st (diagram 94).

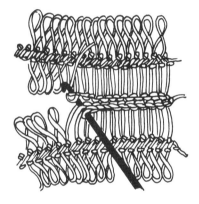

Diagram 94   Joining with a double slip stitch

Surface hairpin crochet

The basic method

Fasten the yarn to the right-hand upright of the hairpin frame, and holding the frame horizontally, wind the yarn round the two upright bars for the required number of loops (diagram 95). Make certain that there are the same number of loops on both uprights, and then tie the yarn to the right-hand upright to secure, and cut, leaving a 10 cm (4 in) end.

Join the yarn over the first loop with a dc, keeping the working end at the back of the frame. Insert the hook over the next double loop y o h, and pull through over the loop and through the loop on the hook. Continue in this way up the frame, making

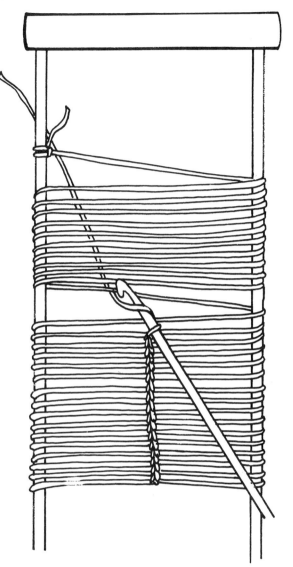

Diagram 95   A surface hairpin strip

certain that the chain remains in the centre of the frame. Cut the yarn leaving a 10 cm (4 in) end and pull it through the last loop. Slip the strip carefully from the frame and work all strips in this way.

To work a fan edge

Wind a multiple of 32 loops (diagram 96).

To work the upper edge

Join on yarn at top right-hand loop with a dc, *1 ch, 1 dc into the next loop and repeat from * into each of

79

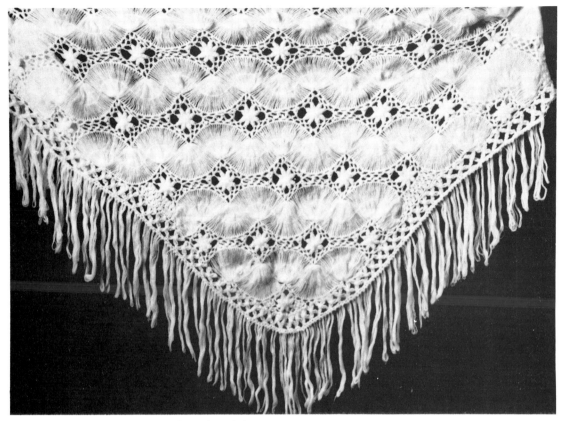

Fig. 43   A hairpin shawl using a surface spine stitch

the next 30 loops, 1 ch, and holding the next 32 loops together work 1 dc; repeat the two sets of 32 loops for the pattern along the row.

To work the lower edge

* 1 dc into the first 32 loops, holding them together, 1 ch, 1 dc into each of the next 32 loops; repeat from * to the end of the strip, fasten off.

To work a shawl (figure 43)

First strip   21 fans of 32 loops
Second strip   15 fans of 32 loops plus ½ fan at each end (i.e. 16 loops)
Third strip   13 fans of 32 loops
Fourth strip   7 fans of 32 loops plus ½ fan at each end (i.e. 16 loops)
Fifth strip   5 fans of 32 loops

To join the strips

Each edge, the top and the lower one, are crocheted with * 1 dc, miss 2 ch, work 3 ch and repeat from * along strip, fasten off. Repeat for each strip, (diagram 97 and figure 44).

The strips are joined by placing the fan top in the first row facing downwards with the fan top in the second row facing upwards directly below it and the large spaces are filled with 8-petal clusters (figure 44) and the chains in the narrow spaces are joined by chains of 3 ch and connected with ss. The side edges are filled with chains of 6 sts connected by a row of crossed trebles. Add a fringe into the last row of chains (diagram 98).

Fig. 44   A detail of the fan surface motifs

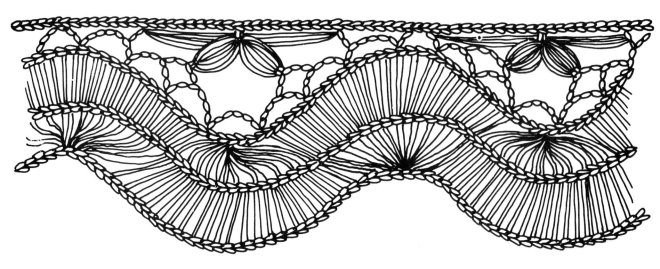

Diagram 96   Working the fan edge

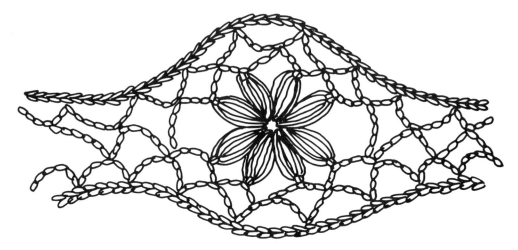

Diagram 97   Joining the strips with chains and detail of
petal clusters

Diagram 98   Working the filling for the side edges

82

8 IRISH CROCHET

Historical background

Irish crochet is one of the most beautiful of all the Irish laces, owing to its fineness of thread in the working of the large number of traditional motifs. The background net connecting these motifs is typical of Irish crochet and is one of its characteristics.

When the convents in France were persecuted during the middle of the nineteenth century, the nuns fled to several neighbouring countries, one of which was Ireland, and continued the skill of lace-making in the schools and convents of that country. This proved to be a great salvation for the Irish people during the Great Famine, as it introduced a new industry which helped the local economy.

An effort was made to imitate the Venetian point lace in crochet, taking advantage of the fact that flax of a good quality was grown on a large scale in Ireland, offering a plentiful supply of linen yarn.

The home industry thus started was successful and flourished mainly in the south and south-west of the country and continued to be taught in the schools in New Ross, Kenmare, Kinsale, Killarney and Clonakilty, but it was in Youghal that the highest standard was reached. The teaching spread over the whole of the country and the demand for the crochet lace finally reached the New World, where the prosperity enjoyed by the people there stimulated its sale.

Since then its popularity has fluctuated, and during the period between the two World Wars there was a notable decline in interest, but during the last two decades its beauty and usefulness have once again been recognised. Fashion designers have in-corporated its motifs into trimmings for blouses, gowns, lingerie, tablemats and cloths.

The large cotton firms have experimented with many new designs, some of which are more properly called Azores crochet, which has many facets of Tenerife lace. In this the Irish crochet influence can be seen combining with that of the sun laces of Spain and Portugal.

The modern work shows a tendency to coarseness owing to the popular demand in fashion, but as its attractiveness is recognised again, there could once more be a return to the delicate tracery of previous work.

The basic method

The best results for the working of Irish crochet are obtained by working with fine cotton, for example Coats mercer cotton No 20, 40 and 60, or DMC No 40, 50 and 60. The crochet hooks used should be correspondingly fine, No 1.25, 1.00 or .75 respectively.

The stitches used are traditionally chain stitch, double crochet, treble, picots and double crochet worked over various strands of cord.

The individual motifs are worked separately, the chosen design being traced onto a sheet of thin tracing paper, and the motifs attached to their selected place with a few tacking threads. When this has been done, and the type of background net has been selected, the motifs are joined together with a chain stitch.

To obtain the flat finish of the background net it is advisable to bend the work backwards at the row being used, in order that there is room for the crochet hook to be manipulated. The work should be frequently inspected for any signs of puckering.

At the completion of this, the work is carefully removed from the paper by cutting away the tacking threads. A picot edging is then worked around the outer edge of the design to give a firm outline, and for the inner edge a finish is obtained by a row of 1 tr, 3 ch, miss 3 stitches of the previous row and repeat along to the end, thus making a finish of spaces and trebles.

Background stitches

Chain lace

Make a chain a little longer than is required.

Row 1 1 dc into the tenth ch from the hook, *6 ch, miss 3 ch, 1 dc into the next ch; repeat from * across the row, 9 ch, turn.

Row 2 * 1 dc into the next loop, repeat from * across the row, ending with 6 ch, 1 dc into the last loop, 9 ch, turn.

Repeat Row 2 for the length required.

Single picot loop

Make a chain a little longer than is required.

Row 1 1 dc into the third ch from the hook (a picot made). 1 ch, 1 dc into the eighth ch from the picot, *3 ch, 1 dc into the third ch from the hook, 4 ch, 1 dc into the third ch from the hook, 1 ch, miss 3 ch, 1 dc into the next ch (picot loop made); repeat from * across the row, 7 ch, turn.

Row 2 1 dc into third ch from the hook, 1 dc between the picots of the first loop, *1 picot loop, 1 dc between the picots of the next loop; repeat from * working the last dc into the loop after the last picot, 7 ch turn.

Repeat Row 2 for the length required.
Fasten off.

Double picot loop

Make a ch a little longer than is required.

Row 1 1 dc into the third ch from the hook, (a picot made). 2 ch, 1 dc into the eighth ch from the picot, *6 ch, 1 dc into the third ch from the hook, 2 ch, miss 4 ch, 1 dc into the next ch; repeat from * across the row, 8 ch, turn.

Row 2 1 dc into the third ch from the hook, 2 ch, 1 dc into the first loop (after the picot), * 6 ch, 1 dc into

the third ch from the hook, 2 ch, 1 dc into the next loop (after the picot); repeat from * across the row, 8 ch, turn.

Repeat Row 2 for the length required.

Loop lace

Make a ch a little longer than is required.

Row 1 1 dc into the fifteenth ch from the hook, 4 ch, 1 dc into the same place, * 10 ch, miss 6 ch, then work 1 dc, 4 ch, and 1 dc into the next ch; repeat from * across the row, turn.

Row 2 Ss to the centre of the 4 ch loop, 13 ch, * into the next 10 ch loop work 1 dc, 4 ch, and 1 dc, 10 ch; repeat from * across the row ending with 1 dc, 4 ch, and 1 dc into the last loop, turn.

Repeat Row 2 for the length required.
Fasten off.

Individual motifs

Leaf

Starting at the tip make 15 ch.

Row 1 1 dc into the second ch from the hook, 1 dc into each ch to within the last ch, 3 dc into the last ch (tip of the leaf). 1 dc into each ch along the opposite side of the foundation ch, 1 dc into the same place as the last dc. Hereafter, only pick up the back loop of each dc; 1 dc into each of the next 11 dc; 1 ch, turn.

Row 2 1 dc into each dc to within the centre dc of the 3 dc group. Into the next dc work 1 dc, 1 ch, and 1 dc; 1 dc into each dc on the other side to within 4 dc from the centre dc at the tip of the leaf, 1 ch, turn.

Row 3 1 dc into each dc to within the 1 ch; into the 1 ch sp work 1 dc, 1 ch, and 1 dc; 1 dc into each dc on the other side to within the last 3 dc; 1 ch, turn.

Row 4 As the third row.

Row 5 As the third row making 7 ch instead of 1 ch.

Row 6 1 dc into each dc to within 7 ch; into the 7 ch loop work 2 dc, 5 ch, 3 dc, 5 ch, 3 dc, 5 ch and 2 dc; 1 dc into each dc on other side of the leaf to within the last 3 dc. Fasten off.

Trefoil

Commence with 15 ch, then join with a ss to form a ring.

Row 1 Working over a cord (or 4 strands of the same thread) make 27 dc into the ring.

Row 2 1 dc into each dc 1 ss into the first dc made and then let the cord hang down.

Row 3 *Make 25 ch; 1 dc into each of the next 9 dc; repeat from * twice more.

Row 4 Working over the cord, *make 33 dc into the next loop, 1 dc into each of the next 9 dc; repeat from * twice more. Cut off the cord.

Row 5 1 ss into the first dc on the loop; *1 dc into the next dc, 4 ch, miss 2 ch; repeat from * 9 times more, 1 dc into the next dc, 1 ss into each dc to within the second dc of the next loop; repeat from the first * twice more.

Row 6 Ss to the centre of the first 4 ch loop, * 2 dc into the same loop; into each of next 8 loops work 2 dc, 3 ch and 2 dc, 2 dc into the next loop, ss to the centre of the first loop on the next petal; repeat from * ending with 2 dc into the last loop on the last leaf of the shamrock, ss to the centre of the section between the petals. Now work 25 ch (for stem), turn, 1 dc into the second ch from hook, 1 dc into each ch, 1 ss into the next st at base of stem and into each of the remaining stitches of the section between the petals. Fasten off.

Flower

Starting at the centre make 20 ch, join with a ss to form a ring.

Round 1 3 ch, work 47 tr into the ring, join with a ss.

Round 2 1 tr into each tr of the previous round. Do not break off.

To work the petals

Row 1 *5 ch, miss 1 st and 1 dc into the next stitch. Repeat from * twice more, 7 ch, turn.

Row 2 to Row 6 *inclusive* 1 dc in the next loop, *5 ch, 1 dc in the next loop. Repeat from * once more, 7 ch, turn. Do not work 7 ch at the end of Row 6.

Row 7 Ss to the centre of the next loop, 5 ch, dc into the next loop, turn.

Row 8 Ss to the centre of the next loop, 8 ch, 1 dc into the next loop. Fasten off.

*Miss 2 tr at the base of the petal, and attach the thread in the next stitch and work another petal. Repeat from * until 6 petals are made.

To attach the thread

Attach the thread between the two free tr between the petals and work over a cord as follows.

Round 1 *1 dc into the same place as where the thread was attached. *4 dc in the first loop, 3 dc in each end loop of the next 6 rows, 11 dc in the loop at the tip of the petal. Work other side to correspond, 1 dc between the two dc at the base of the petals. Repeat from * five times more.
Join and cut off the cord.

Round 2 1 dc in the same place as the ss. *2 ch, miss 2 dc, tr in the next dc. Repeat from * 7 times more , 2 ch, 1 tr in each of the next 7 dc with 2 ch between each, **2 ch, miss 2 dc, 1 tr in the next dc. Repeat from ** 6 times more, 2 ch, dc in the dc between the petals

To work the remaining five petals

Round 3 Ss to the third space, and working over the padding, make 3 dc in the space, *work 3 dc, 3 ch, and 3 dc closely over padding alone, miss 1 space, 3 dc in the next space. Repeat from * 8 times more; 3 dc in the third space of the next petal and work in this manner around. Join and fasten off.

Scroll

Row 1 Work 67 ch, turn, ss in the sixteenth ch from the hook.

Row 2 Working over 4 strands make 2 dc in each of next 15 sts, then dc in each st across to within the last 15 sts, then work 2 dc in each of the remaining sts, ss in the sixteenth ch from the hook on the foundation ch. Cut off the cord, turn.

Row 3 * miss 1 dc, 1 tr into each of the next 2 dc, 1 ch. Repeat from * to within the last dc, 3 ch, miss the next dc, ss in the next ss and turn (33 spaces).

Row 4 *Make 4 tr in the next space; in the following space make 2 dc, 3 ch, dc in the third ch from the hook, (picot) 2 dc in the same space, miss 2 tr. Repeat from * 4 times more, 4 dc in the next space, ** 4 dc in each of the next 2 spaces, 2 dc in the next space, 8 ch, turn; miss 7 dc, ss in the next dc, turn; 4 dc in the 8 ch loop, 3 ch, picot, 3 dc in the same loop, 3 ch, picot, 4 dc in the same loop, 2 dc in the same space where the 8 ch loop started; in the next loop make 2 dc, picot, 2 dc. Repeat from ** once more, make another solid picot loop and finish the other end of the scroll to correspond. Fasten off.

Rose

Commence with 8 ch, join with a ss to form a ring.

Row 1 6 ch, *1 tr into the ring, 3 ch; repeat from * 4 times more, 1 ss into the third of the 6 ch.

Row 2 Into each sp work 1 dc, 1 hlf tr, 3 tr, 1 hlf tr and 1 dc (6 petals).

Row 3 * 5 ch, 1 dc into the next tr of the row before the last, inserting the hook from the back; repeat from * ending with 5 ch.

Row 4 Into each sp work 1 dc, 1 hlf tr, 5 tr, 1 hlf tr and 1 dc.

Row 5 *7 ch, 1 dc into the next dc of the row before the last, inserting the hook from the back; repeat from * ending with 7 ch.

Row 6 Into each sp work 1 dc, 1 hlf tr, 7 tr, 1 hlf tr and 1 dc, 1 ss into the first dc. Fasten off.

Shamrock

Commence with 16 ch.

Row 1 1 dc into the sixteenth ch from the hook, 15 ch, 1 dc into the same ch, 15 ch, 1 dc into the same ch.

Row 2 22 dc into each loop.

Row 3 1 dc into each dc missing the first and the last dc on each petal, 25 ch, turn (so starting stem).

Row 4 1 dc into the second ch from the hook, 1 dc into each ch, 1 ss into the first dc on the next petal. Fasten off.

Thistle

Take two strands of padding thread. Fasten the thread to the end and work 5 dc over it. Then join with a ss to form a circle and draw up very tightly.

Now work a dc into the back of the dc and over the thread, putting 2 dc into every dc of the previous row and continue this for 5 rows. The 2 dc will not be required in every stitch, but simply enough to lie flat. Let padding thread lie loosely, and then work 18 ch, ss to the next dc of the circle and work 10 dc over the ch, * 8 ch, ss to the next dc of the circle and work 10 dc over it. Repeat from * three times. Work 1 dc between each group of dc right over the top of the thistle and then 10 dc into the 18 ch. Pass the padding thread at the back of the motif, directly opposite the 10 ch at the top. Work 8 dc over it and into the back of the dc at the circle, turn, work 6 dc into the centre of the 8 dc, turn, work 4 dc into the centre of the 6 dc, and then work 24 dc over the thread for the stem.

Daisy

Wind the thread four times around the end of a pencil, then into the ring work 20 dc and join the last dc to the first dc with a ss. Work 1 dc into the last ss, then make * 6 ch, miss 1 dc of the previous row and work 1 dc into next st. Repeat from * all round 9 times more, join with a ss. Into each loop work 1 dc, 6 tr, and 1 dc.

Fig. 45   A late nineteenth century collar

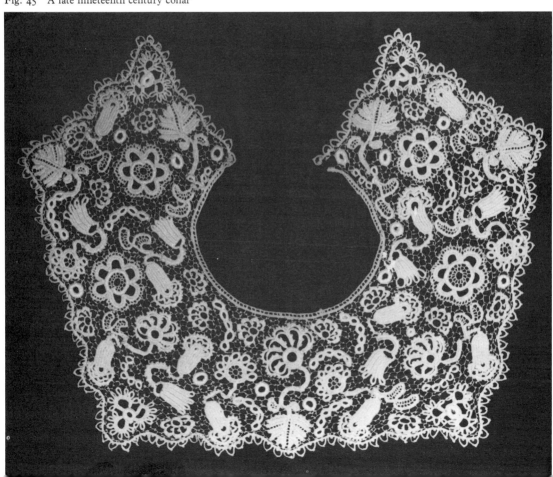

Roll stitch

This stitch is known by various names, coil st or bullion st amongst them.

To work the roll st

A medallion using a roll st commences with 8 ch, ss into first ch to form a ring. Wind the thread around the hook 10 times, insert the hook into the ring already made, and pull through a loop. Holding the thread firmly and controlling the group with the middle finger of the right hand, take the thread over the hook, through the loop and the coil on the hook. Hold in position with the finger and work 1 ch into the loop on the hook, meanwhile drawing the thread up at the back of the coil and having it even with it.

Row 1 Make 8 coils into the ring altogether, and with having 5 ch between each pair and starting with 5 ch to be concealed behind the first coil.

Row 2 Work 6 dc into each space.

Row 3 Work 1 dc into each of the next 6 dc, turn, miss the first dc, 1 dc into each of the following dc. Repeat this row, missing the first dc in each row until there is only one dc in the top of the pyramid, then work a ss to the next dc on the centre ring and repeat from *. Work a row of dc over the edges of the pyramids all round and join the motifs in two points at each side whilst working the last row if required.

Clones knot

To make a medium size knot, commence with 7 ch and draw up the loop on the hook for 2.5 cm (1 in) from the point. Then place the middle finger on it to keep this in place whilst looping the thread over the hook above the ch, then below the ch alternately until the ch up to the first st is covered with the loops. These must be kept close together and even. Now insert the hook into the first ch, then take the thread over the needle and through all the loops on the hook, twisting the hook around slowly so as to let it pass smoothly through the loops. Make a ch through the loop on the hook, pulling up the knot tightly. Finish the knot with a dc around the stem of the knot. The convex side of the knot is the right side and this is secured with a dc into the centre on which the knot is made.

Fig. 46   A tray cloth

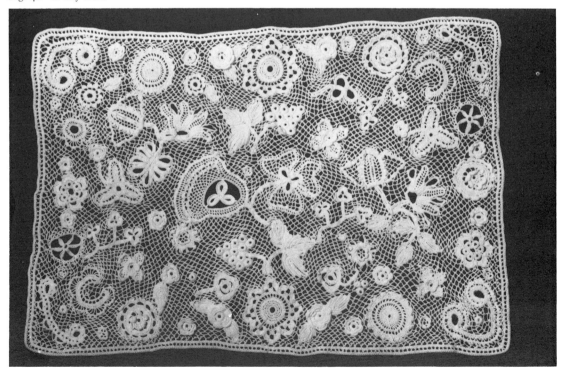

Wheel

Commence with 8 ch, join with a ss to form a ring. Working over a cord, or four strands of thread, make 18 dc into the ring.

Rows 2–6 1 dc into each dc increasing 6 dc at equal distances apart (to increase, work 2 dc into 1 dc). Cut off the cord, then work 1 ss into the next dc. Fasten off.

Flowerette

Starting at the centre make 15 ch, and join with a ss.

Round 1 Work 26 dc into the ring and join with a ss.

Round 2 Work 4 ch, * 1 tr in the next dc, 1 ch. Repeat from * around and join to the third of the 4 ch first made (26 sp).

Round 3 2 dc into each sp all round and join with a ss (52 dc).

Round 4 Work 1 tr into each dc all round, increasing 8 tr in the round by making 2 tr in each increase. Join with a ss (60 tr).

Round 5 Work 1 dc into the same place as the last ss, * 2 ch, miss 2 sts, 1 tr in the next st, 2 ch, 1 trip tr into each of the next 5 sts, and working 2 ch between each trip tr; 2 ch, 1 dbl tr in the next st, 2 ch, miss 2 sts, dc in the next st. Repeat from * all round (5 fans).

Round 6 *Work 2 dc in the next sp; in each of the next 6 sps make 2 dc, 3 ch, 2 dc; work 2 dc in the next sp. Repeat from * all round. Join with a ss into the first dc. Break off.

Grape and vine

To make a bunch of grapes

Wind the thread 4 times around a knitting needle of medium size, slip this off the needle and into the ring work double crochet as closely as possible. Join the first and last dc with a ss. Make 11 more buttons like this and sew together in a formation of one at the bottom, then two above followed by three, then four above. The last two to be sewn one on each side of the stem.

To make the stem

This is made by covering 4 cm ($1\frac{1}{2}$ in) of padding with dc. Turn, work another row of dc on top of this, draw into the required shape and sew to the bunch of grapes.

To make the vine leaf

This is made in three sections. First of all work 4 cm ($1\frac{1}{2}$ in) of chain, then work a row of dc (over 6 rows of padding) down both sides of it, making as many dc at the turn as is necessary to lie flat. Work another row

Fig. 47 Rose and trefoil motifs

Fig. 48   An antique collar

Fig. 49   A section of the collar

Fig. 50   A point of the collar showing the unusual clone picot chain background

Fig. 51   An antique collar dominated by its butterfly motifs

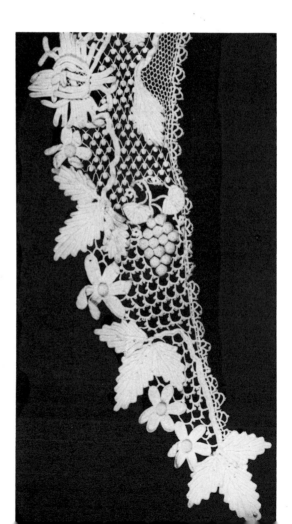

of dc on top of the first row, until about 3 sts from the end, then work 2 dc on the padding alone, turn, work a row of dc on top of this last row (1 rib). Work another rib on the other side and continue working until there are two ribs on each side of the centre one; fasten off.

Make two more in the same way, sew them together, sew a button on the centre and work a stem as before, sewing it up into a circle at one end. Fasten the other end to the leaf with a few strong stitches. This completes the pattern.

Coiled loops

Commence with a long piece of four-fold padding cord and fasten the working thread into the folded end with 1 dc, then working over the cord throughout form 20 dc, then fasten into a ring by working 1 dc into the first dc; pull the end of the cord to make the ring firm. * Work 25 dc after the ring, and fasten to the fifth dc on the ring with 1 dc, turning the cord first to the right, upwards towards the left to form a coil.

90

Fig. 52   Detail of the butterfly design

Continue over the cord with 10 dc and fasten to the tenth dc of the twenty-fifth dc. Repeat from * keeping the cord slightly pulled so that all the coils may be of equal size.

A late nineteenth century collar is shown in figure 45 and this combines most of the motifs in this chapter.

In the design for a tray cloth *(figure 46)*, the rose motif is shown in several positions together with a repeat motif of vine and grapes, and a selection of wheels to balance. All are shown against a chain background.

In figure 47 a traditional rose square is shown joined to a trefoil square.

The antique collar in figure 48 is a beautiful example of Irish crochet, using bold motifs of leaves and flowers. Here again are the bunches of grapes with leaves, the former being very well padded. An unusual background is seen in the detail at the neckline in figure 49, where strength is shown by the chain stitch against the mixture of single picot chains and clone stitch chains.

The collar in figure 51 shows the well-balanced placing of the flower and leaf motifs and emphasises the butterflies at each corner. The chain of rose motifs adds strength at the neckline.

The detail of this collar *(figure 52)* shows in clear contrast the butterfly motifs against the simplicity of a chain background.

9 TAMBOUR CROCHET EMBROIDERY

Historical background

The definition of tambour crochet is embroidery in chain stitch done by means of a small hook. The roots of tambour embroidery go back many thousands of years to China, where exquisite work was done in silk threads. Eventually the craft found its way through India, Persia and into Turkey, where it remained for a long time only for use in the harems. Its designs were for the decoration of veils and garments. It became a mixture of tambour and crochet known as Oyah lace. In general it was still called tambour because of the frame on which the material was stretched. This was like a half-egg-shaped drum, and held between the knees. This method continued until, at the beginning of the nineteenth century,

tambour embroidery was worked on net in Coggeshall, a village in Essex, in imitation of French lace. It was of a very high quality and after a lapse during the war years has again reached this high standard, and is known as Coggeshall Lace. Tambour (crochet) embroidery has also adapted itself to the modern tastes, in as much that garments are once again decorated with its geometric designs in bold colours.

Figure 53 shows a delicate tray design worked in tambour lace, using stitches with the delightful names of bold smuggler, spot, neat, and honeycomb for the petals of hellebores. This, with many other imaginative ideas, are found in Jean Dudding's book *Creating Coggeshall Lace*.

Another exquisite example is the tablemat, one of a set, showing casket shapes with decorative fillings *(figure 54)*.

Fig. 53   A tray design of twentieth century Coggeshall lace

Fig. 54 One of a set of tablemats showing casket shapes with decorative fillings

Materials

Any materials with the mesh wide enough to allow the hook to pass through without breaking the threads will be satisfactory. Use an embroidery hoop, or a tapestry frame, but with an embroidery hoop always bind the rim with a soft material. The only other thing you will need is a tambour needle.

The basic stitch

1. Draw the design onto the material: place a section in the hoop, pulling it taut *(diagram 99)*.
2. The thread is held in the left hand underneath the hoop. Starting at one side of the design, put the hook through the material to the back of the frame. Catch the thread on the hook, and leaving a 10 cm (4 in) tail, bring it through to the front. Make the loop slightly longer than the stitch required to prevent puckering. To secure the tail thread at the beginning wrap the end around the hook, draw it through the back of the first stitch and make a knot *(diagram 100)*.
3. Hold the loop on the hook and put the hook again through the material in the line of the design to the back of the frame. Press the material down when pulling the thread through for the next stitch. Pull

the thread up through the material and the first loop, making a chain stitch *(diagram 101)*.

It is important that the loops making the outline are the same distance apart and that the threads making the loops are always of even tension. To fill in a motif, or to make an allover design, work the rows of the stitches close together.

When the design is completed, disengage the hook. Insert it from the back and pull the last loop through to the back. Cut off the thread, leaving a long enough tail to tie and neaten off.

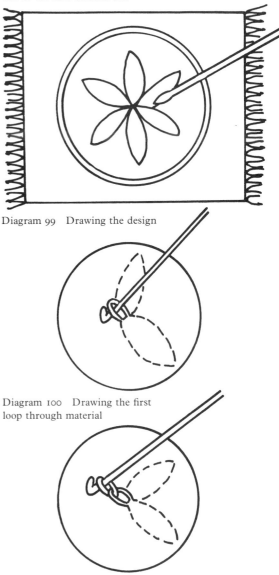

Diagram 99   Drawing the design

Diagram 100   Drawing the first loop through material

Diagram 101   Pulling through the second loop of chain

10 TUNISIAN CROCHET

Historical background

As the name implies, this technique is peculiar to North Africa. It probably developed from knitting, which it resembles, and centuries ago it was only worked by men of the nomad tribes.

It is difficult to obtain the precise dating of its development owing to the fact that it was worked mainly in wool, which unfortunately deteriorates with wear and so the patterns were lost. The nights in the desert were cold and the wool from the herds of sheep and goats were the most natural commodity to hand for warmth.

The tool with which the work is made is the length of a knitting needle, but with a hook at one end; thus in the picking up row it resembles knitting, by having all the stitches on one needle. However, in the second row, which is the take off, or return row, it has the appearance of crochet, where the stitches are taken off, leaving one behind. The patterns and the colours are still traditional, bold in colour, taken from the surrounding landscape and reflecting the light and shade of the desert.

The wares are, traditionally, bags, belts, mats, wall hangings and caps, similar to those worn by the men, with geometric designs.

The basic method

Tunisian stitch differs from ordinary crochet in that the hook is held from above and not as one would hold a pen, and the movement is more by the left than by the right hand.

With the Tunisian hook make a chain of the required number of stitches.

First Foundation Row Insert the hook into the second chain from the hook, wind the yarn over the hook and draw the loop through. Place this loop on the hook together with the one already there. Insert the hook into the next foundation stitch, wind the yarn over the hook, draw the loop through and place it on the hook together with the other loops (*diagram 102*). Repeat this pulling up of the loops and keep them on the hook to the end of the row. There should now be the same number of loops on the hook as there were cast on for the chain.

Do not turn the work.

Second Foundation Row Wind the yarn over the hook and draw it through the first loop only. * After this wind the yarn over the hook and draw it through the next two loops, repeating from * along the row, leaving one loop on the hook (*diagram 103*).

Diagram 102   Picking up the loops from the chain

Diagram 103   Taking off the loops in pairs

These two Foundation Rows form the basis of the pattern rows and the work is not turned (see below).

Purl

Bring the yarn forward and hold with the left thumb below the bar to be worked. Insert the hook under this bar and draw up a loop.

Decreasing

To form a point decrease at each end *(diagram 105)*. One stitch is decreased at each end of every row. On the pick up row the first 2 bars are joined together by inserting the hook through both; wind the yarn over the hook and draw through both loops. Continue along the row, leaving the last two bars on the left hand. These are now taken together when working the return row. Continue to the end of the row.

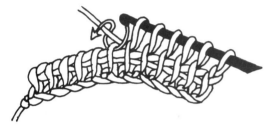

Diagram 104   The second pick up row

Diagram 105   Working a decrease

Increasing

These are made first at the right-hand side and then at the left hand of the same row. To make an increase, the first stitch is made through the bar in the usual manner, followed by inserting the hook into the horizontal bar after the first stitch. Continue along the row until reaching the last bar. Insert the hook into the horizontal bar before the last vertical bar, yarn over hook, and pull up the extra stitch. Com-

Fig. 55   Tunisian simple stitch

plete the last stitch.

Stitch variations

Tunisian simple

Work the length of chain necessary, followed by the two foundation rows.

Row 1   * Insert the hook under the next vertical thread from right to left, wind the yarn over the hook and draw the loop through; repeat from * to the end of the row, leaving all the loops on the hook.
Do not turn the work.
Row 2   1 chain, then * wind yarn over the hook, draw through 2 loops; repeat from * to the end of the row, leaving 1 loop on the hook.
Do not turn the work. Repeat the last 2 rows for the pattern *(figure 55 and diagram 104)*.

Tunisian cellular

Work the length of chain required followed by the 2 foundation rows.

Row 1   * Insert the hook through the horizontal loops at the back of the bar and repeat from * along the row *(figure 56)*.
Row 2   Repeat Row 2 of Tunisian simple. Do not turn.

96

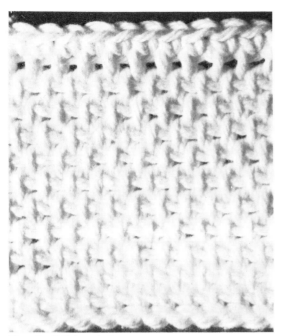

Fig. 56   Cellular stitch

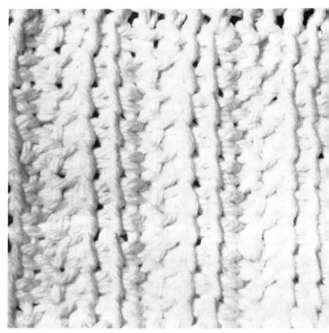

Fig. 57   Ribbing with plain and purl stitch

Ribbing

Make a chain of the required number of stitches.
Work 2 foundation rows.
Row 1   Work a row in rib of 2 purl, and 2 plain.
Row 2   Take off 2 loops at a time to the end of the
row as in the basic stitch.

To work the purl stitch

Keep the yarn in front of the work. Insert the hook
through the next vertical bar, wind the yarn over the
hook, and draw through the bar together with the
preceding yarn-over. This, together with the loop
already on the hook, makes the first 2 purl.

To work the plain stitch

* Insert the hook through the next vertical bar
together with the next horizontal bar, yarn over hook,
and draw through both of the loops. Repeat from *
once more for the 2 plain of the rib *(figure 57)*.

Puff stitch

Make a chain to the multiple of 8.
Work 2 foundation rows.

Rows 1 and 2   Repeat the 2 foundation rows twice
more.
Row 3   Pick up the first 2 bars, work 1 twisted
cluster in the next bar and in the corresponding loop
of the first foundation row; * pick up each of the next
7 bars and work 1 twisted cluster in the next bar and
the corresponding loop of the foundation row; repeat
from * to the end of the row.
Work the take off row.
Row 4   Pick up the first 2 bars, * 1 cluster into the
top of the twisted cluster, pick up each of the next 7
bars and repeat from * to the end of the row.
Work the take off row.
Row 5   *Work 1 cluster in the next bar and the
corresponding bar of the previous pick up row. Pick
up each of the following 3 bars and repeat from * to
the end of the row. Work the take off row.
Row 6   Repeat Row 4 and the take off row.
Repeat from the foundation rows for the pattern.

To work the twisted cluster

Make the required number of chain.
Work 3 foundation rows.
Row 4   Pick up each of the first two bars, yarn over
hook, insert hook in the third pick up loop directly

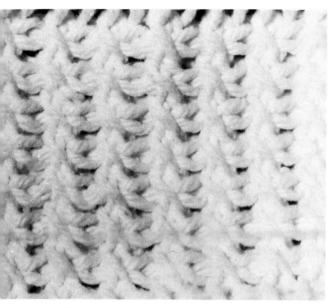

Fig. 58   Cross stitch

below, yarn over hook and pull up a long loop, yarn over hook and take through last 2 loops. Repeat from * to the end of the row.

Cross stitch

Work the required number of chain.
Follow this with 2 foundation rows and proceed with 2 rows of pattern.

Row 1   *Missing 1 vertical thread, insert the hook from right to left under the following vertical thread, yarn over hook, and draw loop through. Insert the hook from right to left under the missed vertical thread, yarn over hook and draw loop through; repeat from * to the end of the row.

Row 2   1 chain, then * yarn over hook, draw through 2 loop on the hook; repeat from * to the end of the row, leaving 1 loop on the hook *(figure 58)*.

Fancy Tunisian stitch

Work the required number of chain and follow this with the 2 rows of the foundation pattern. The next 2 rows are the pattern rows.

Row 1   Insert hook into the horizontal stitch at the back of the second upright stitch of the previous row, draw yarn through, * insert hook into the horizontal stitch at the back of the next upright stitch and draw

the yarn through. Repeat from * to the end of the row.

Row 2   Yarn over hook, draw through the first loop on hook, *yarn over hook, draw through 2 loops on hook, repeat from * to the end of the row.

Mussel stitch

Make a chain to the required length.

Row 1   Pull up a loop through the chain, yarn over the hook, and draw up another loop through the same stitch. Make a similar group of stitches in every other stitch of the chain.

Row 2   First, draw through 3 loops; make 1 ch, yarn over the hook, and draw through the chain stitch first made and the group of 3 stitches at the same time; repeat to the end of the row.

In working every row corresponding to the first row, always draw through the top loop of each chain stitch of the preceeding row.

Houndstooth

Work with 2 colours, A and B.
With A make an uneven number of chain, and work 2 rows of basic Tunisian stitch.

Row 1   Drop A, join B and with the latter draw up a loop in the first space (between the first 2 uprights) and in each space to the last space, miss the last space and draw up a loop in the last vertical bar.

Row 2   Work off loops as in Tunisian plain. Drop B and pick up A.

Row 3   With A miss thfe first space, and draw up a loop in each space to the end; draw up a loop in the last bar.

Row 4   Work off the loops as in Tunisian plain.
Repeat Rows 1 and 2 for the pattern.

Plaited stitch

Work a length of chain divisible by 2, then work Row 1 of the simple Tunisian, followed by the return row.

Row 1   Insert the hook from right to left through the third upright stitch, draw the yarn through, insert the hook through the second upright stitch, draw the yarn through, * miss one upright stitch, insert the hook through the next upright stitch, draw the yarn through, insert the hook through the stitch that was missed, draw the yarn through, and repeat from * until one upright stitch remains. Insert the hook through this stitch, and draw the yarn through.

Row 2   Yarn over the hook, draw through the first

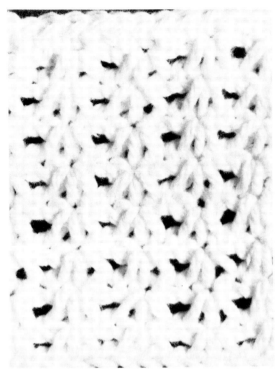

Fig. 59   Shell stitch

loop on the hook, * yarn over the hook and draw
through two loops on the hook, repeat from * to the
end of the row.
Repeat Row 1 for the length required.

Shell pattern

Work a chain divisible by 3 and 2 over.

Row 1   Miss first chain, * insert hook into next
chain, draw yarn through and keep the loop on the
hook, repeat from * to the end of the row.

Row 2   * 2 chain, then yarn over the hook, and draw
through 4 loops on the hook, repeat from * until 2
loops remain on the hook, 1 chain, yarn over the
hook, draw through the remaining 2 loops.

Row 3   Insert the hook into the 1 chain last worked,
draw the yarn through and keep the loop on the hook,
* insert the hook into the small horizontal stitch at the
top back of the next group of loops, draw the yarn
through and keep the loop on the hook, insert the
hook into the first of the 2 chain worked between the
loops, draw the yarn through and keep the loop on the
hook. Insert the hook into the next chain, draw the
yarn through and keep the loop on the hook, repeat
from * to the end of the row.

Next row   Repeat as for Row 2 *(figure 59)*.

Gobelin

Work a loose chain of the length required.

Row 1   Take up each stitch of the foundation row,
taking the yarn over the hook each time before taking
up a stitch.

Row 2   Work back in Tunisian stitch, drawing
through three loops at the same time.

Row 3   Make a chain stitch when beginning only,
and work as in Row 1, taking up the loops of what
looks like a chain running underneath the upright
stitches. Work back as before.

Raised Puff

Make 2 rows of plain Tunisian stitch of the required
length.

Row 3   Take up 3 stitches in plain Tunisian; yarn
over the hook, and draw a loop up through the fourth
stitch in Row 1; yarn over the hook and draw through
2 stitches, leaving the last stitch made on the hook;
yarn over the hook and draw a loop through as before;
yarn over the hook, work through 2 stitches, wind
yarn over again and through 2 more loops, thus
making a treble crochet; make 3 more trebles in the
same stitch, always leaving the last stitch made on the
hook. Omit, or pass the stitch under the puff; begin
with the one next to it and take up 5 stitches; then
begin the next puff and finish it the same as the
preceeding one. Work back as in plain Tunisian.

Row 4   Make one row of plain Tunisian.

Row 5   Take up the stitches the same as in Row 3,
arranging the puffs so that they will alternate.

Sleeveless jacket in lace stitch

Materials
Double knitting yarn 14 (15, 16) 25 g balls (12 oz)
Tunisian crochet hook 5.00 mm
Crochet hook 3.50 mm
Tapestry needle
Measurements
Bust 86 (91, 97) cm 34 (36, 38) in
Length from shoulder 65 (66, 67) cm, $25\frac{1}{2}$ (26, $26\frac{1}{2}$)
   in
Tension over lace stitch
9 stitches to 5 cm (2 in)

To work the back

Cast on with the Tunisian hook 80 (88, 96) stitches.
** Work 2 rows of basic foundation.

Row 1   Miss the first ch from the hook, draw up a
loop in each ch to the end of the row. (Forward row).

Row 2 * Work 3 ch, yarn over the hook, and draw through 5 loops, 1 ch, for the eye and repeat from * to the end of the row. (Return row).

Row 3 * Draw up a loop in the eye, draw up a loop in each of the 3 ch; repeat from * ending with draw up a loop in each of the last 3 ch.

Row 4 Repeat Row 2.

Rows 5 and 6 Repeat Rows 3 and 4 for the pattern until the work measures 44 cm ($17\frac{1}{2}$ in) from the beginning, ending with Row 4. **

To work the armhole shaping

Slip stitch over the first 9 loops, work in pattern across the row until there are 9 loops from the end of the row. Do not turn the work. Pattern back across the row.

Work straight in pattern for 20 (21, 23) cm, 8 ($8\frac{1}{2}$, 9) in, from the beginning of the armhole, ending on Row 4.

To work the shoulders

Slip stitch in pattern over the first 10 loops. Do not turn the work and pattern back. Slip stitch over the first 14 loops and work across the row. Pattern back across the next row, and fasten off.

To work the left front

Cast on 43 (45, 47) chain.
Work as for the instructions given for the back from ** to **.

To work the armhole shaping

Slip stitch across the first 9 loops, pattern across the row until there are 34 (36, 38) loops on the hook and then work back. Continue with the pattern keeping the work straight without decreasing until the work measures 11 (12, 14) cm, 4 (5, $5\frac{1}{2}$) in, from the beginning of the armhole, ending with Row 4.

To work the neck shaping

Slip stitch over the first 12 (12, 14) loops. Pattern to the end of the row until there are 22 (24, 26) loops on the hook, then work back across these stitches. Work straight until the armhole is the same depth as the back, up to the beginning of the shoulder shaping, ending with Row 4.

To work the shoulder shaping

Slip stitch over the first 10 loops, pattern to the end of the row, then work back.
Fasten off.

To work the right front

Work 43 (45, 47) ch.
Work as for the back instructions from ** to **.
Work in pattern across the row until there are 34 (36, 38) loops on the hook, then work back. Work straight for 11 (12, 14) cm, 4 (5, $5\frac{1}{2}$) in, from the beginning of the armhole, ending with Row 4.

To work the neck shaping

Slip stitch over the first 12 (12, 14) loops; pattern to the end of the row (22, 24, 26 loops on the hook) then work back.
Work straight until the armhole is the same depth as the back armholes up to the beginning of the shoulder shaping, ending with Row 4.

To work the shoulder

Pattern until there are 13 (15, 17) loops left on the hook then work back. Fasten off.

To complete

Join the shoulder seams and then the side seams.

Edgings

With right side facing, join the yarn to the right front at the lower edge and work a row of dc all round the outer edge, working a dc over each vertical loop and 1 dc into each ch.

Row 2 1 ch, 1 dc into each dc to the end; slip stitch into the first dc.
Fasten off and finish each armhole in the same way.

To work a Tunisian cover

Materials
Aran or double knitting yarn
A Tunisian hook number 5.50 mm
An embroidery needle and yarn in contrasting
  colours.

Measurements
101 cm (48 in) × 152 cm (60 in)

Method

With the yarn cast on 192 sts to measure 101 cm (48 in).

In Tunisian simple, work 192 rows and cast off.

To work the embroidered design

First of all trace the chosen design onto graph paper

Diagram 106   Working the embroidery stitch

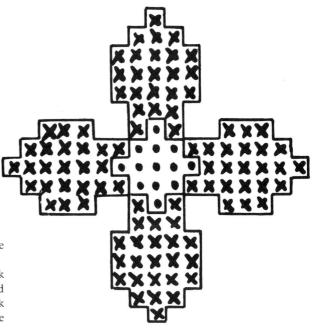

Diagram 107   A design for the small Tunisian squares

and with the needle and coloured yarn follow the design square by square.

Each upright bar across the row of the work represents 1 cross stitch. Starting from the left hand side, join the yarn on the wrong side of the work where the design commences at the lower hole of the first bar and work across the next vertical bar to the upper hole. Bring the needle through the lower hole directly below. Continue to work the number of stitches required for the colour being used. Then work from right to left to form a cross *(diagram 106)*.

A cover in squares

Materials
Yarn 4 ply
Tunisian hook number 4.50 mm
Tapestry needle
Measurements
Size of cover 122 cm (48 in) × 183 cm (72 in)
Size of square with motif, 20.5 cm (8 in) × 20.5 cm (8 in)
Tension
$4\frac{1}{2}$ stitches – 2.5 cm (1 in)
9 stitches – 5 cm (2 in)
36 stitches – 20.5 cm (8 in)

To work a single motif

Cast on a chain of 36 stitches and continue in basic Tunisian stitch for 36 rows.

Neaten all ends and lightly press.

Trace the design onto graph paper and, following this diagram, mark the centre vertical bar for the starting point and work the cross stitches over the vertical bars as previously explained in working the larger cover. Taking care to keep the Tunisian stitches in the same direction, sew the squares together *(diagram 107)*.

To work the edging

With the right side facing attach the yarn to the upper right-hand corner, work 1 ch, ⋆ 3 dc in the same corner, miss 1 vertical bar, 1 dc in next stitch. Repeat dc across the row to the next corner, working from ⋆ to the end of the round, join with a slip stitch. Finish another row with crab stitch putting 3 dc into each corner. Join with a slip stitch into the first dc. Fasten off and lightly press with a damp cloth.

A clutch bag

Materials
5 × 25 g (4 oz) of 4 ply yarn
A Tunisian hook number 3.50 mm
46 cm (18 in) for lining
2 large press fasteners
Measurements when finished
24.2 cm ($9\frac{1}{2}$ in) × 20.43 cm ($8\frac{1}{2}$ in)

To work the bag

Work 58 chain to measure 24.2 cm (9½ in).
Insert the hook into the second chain from the hook, draw a loop through, and continue to draw up all the loops of the chain.

Row 1 Put the yarn round the hook, pull through one loop, ★ yarn round the hook, draw through 2 loops, and repeat from ★ until one loop remains on the hook.

Row 2 Draw a stitch through the vertical loops formed by the stitches of the row beneath.

Rows 3 and 4 Repeat Rows 1 and 2, and these four rows form the pattern.

Continue until the work measures 57.3 cm (22½ in). Fasten off *(diagram 108)*.

To make the sides (2)

Make a chain of 12 stitches.
Insert the hook into the second ch from the hook, draw a loop through and continue to draw up the loops in the chain. Repeat the 4 rows of the pattern until the work measures 17.8 (7 in), then decrease 1 stitch at each end of the following 4 rows. Cast off.

To make up the bag

Lightly press all the pieces with a damp cloth and cut the lining fabric allowing an extra 13 mm (½ in) for seams all round. Cut the canvas to the same measurements as the main piece and tack to the crocheted part.

Mark each side of the main part at 17.8 cm (7 in), at 20.43 cm (8¼ in) and finally at 56.3 cm (22½ in) from the foundation edge.

Join one row end edge of each side piece to each side of main part from the foundation edge to the first markings. Join the lower edge of each side piece to side edges of the main part between the first and second markings. Then join the other row end edges of the side pieces to the side edges of the main part between the second and third markings.

Make up the lining by turning in all edges 13 mm (½ in), pinning into position on the crochet work and slip stitching into place. Work 1 row of dc all round

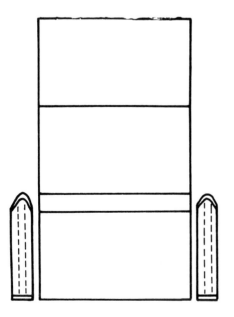

Diagram 108 Layout of the clutch bag

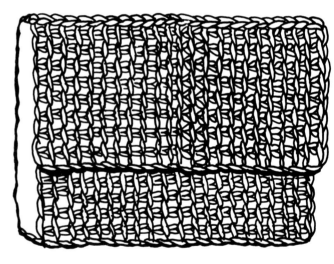

Diagram 109 Completing the clutch bag

the edges and finish with 1 row of crab stitch. Fasten a large press stud at each side of flap to complete *(diagram 109)*.

Star stitch

Make a chain a multiple of 2 plus 1

Rows 1, 2 and 3   Basic Tunisian stitch.

Row 4   2 ch, draw up a loop in the second ch from the hook and in the first 3 bars, y o h, and through 5 loops, 1 ch, (eye) ★ draw up a loop in the centre of the eye, draw up a loop in the back of the last loop picked up, draw up a loop in each of the next 2 bars, y o h, and take through 5 loops, 1 ch, (eye) repeat from ★ to the end. 2 ch, turn.

Row 5   Work 2 hlf tr in the eye of each star, ending with 1 hlf tr in the last st.

Repeat from Row 1 for the pattern, working the first row of loops in each hlf tr *(figure 60)*.

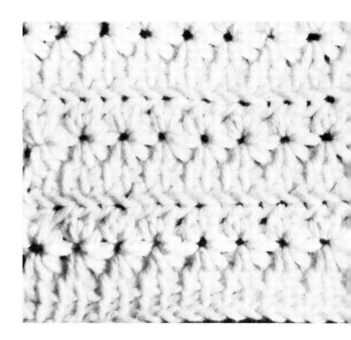

Fig. 60   Star stitch

Fig. 61   Limpet stitch

Limpet stitch

Row 1 4 tr in the fourth ch from the hook, *miss 3 ch, 1 dc in the next ch, miss 3 ch, 1 tr in the next ch, repeat from * to the last 4 ch miss 3 ch, 5 tr in the last ch. 1 ch, turn.

Row 2 (Tunisian stitch), 1 dc in the first tr, * (draw up a loop in the next st and keep the loop on the hook) 5 times (6 loops on the hook) draw up a loop in the next st and draw this loop through the first loop on the hook, forming an upright st or a bar, (y o h and through 2 loops) 5 times *. There are 6 bars and 1 loop on the hook. ** Hold loops on the hook and draw up a loop in each of the next 5 bars (6 loops on hook) draw up a loop in the next stitch and through the first loop on hook (y o h and through 2 loops) 5 times, repeat from ** twice. Insert hook in the second bar, y o h, and through the bar and the loop on hook (first cast off) cast off 4 more st, 1 dc in the next st, repeat from * ending cast off 5 stitches, ss in the top of the turning ch, 1 ch, turn.

Row 3 Miss the first stitch, 1 dc in each st across, ss in the last st. 3 ch, turn.

Row 4 y o h, draw up a loop in the second dc, y o h, and through 2 loops on the hook, (y o h and draw up a loop in the next st, y o h, and through 2 loops) 3 times, y o h and through 5 loops on the hook, 1 ch tightly to form the eye, of $\frac{1}{2}$ shell, * 3 ch, 1 dc in the next stitch, 3 ch, (y o h, and draw up loop in the next st, y o h and through 2 loops) 9 times, y o h and through 10 loops on the hook, 1 ch tightly to form the eye of the full shell; repeat from * ending the last repeat (y o h, and draw up the loop in the next st, y o h, and through 2 loops) 4 times, y o h, and through 5 loops 1 ch tightly to form the eye. 3 ch, turn.

Row 5 4 tr in the eye of the first $\frac{1}{2}$ shell, 1 dc in the first dc, * 9 tr in the eye of the next shell, 1 dc in the next dc; repeat from * ending 5 tr in the eye of the last shell, 1 ch, turn.

Repeat Rows 2 to 5 for the pattern *(figure 61)*.

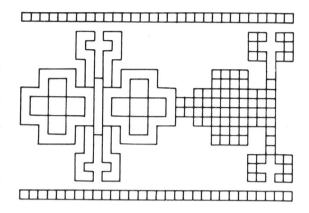

Diagrams 110 & 111   Two designs to work on the flap of the clutch bag

CROCHET SHORTHAND

UK

- ch

- dc

- tr

- hlf tr

- dbl tr

- trip tr

- quad tr

- quin tr

- joint trip tr

- joint cluster

- joint 2 dbl tr cl

- joint 5 dbl tr cl

- pct

- ss

- commence here

USA

- ch

- sc

- half dc

- double cr (dc)

- trip cr (tc)

- dbl trip cr (d t c)

- trip trip cr (t t c)

- Working from the front around stitch

- Working around the st from back

- Make st longer than usual

EUROPEAN

◯	ch
✛	dc
T	half tr
⊤̅	tr
⊤̿	dbl tr
⊤̿	trip tr
●	ss
⋒	pct
Ⱥ	3 joint tr
⋈	joint cluster
◊	leaf cluster
◺	sail cluster
⅄	crossed tr into base st
⅏	relief tr FRONT
⅏	relief tr BACK

 Solomon's knot

crossed tr into middle of st

JAPANESE

◯	h
✛	dc
T	half tr
⊤̅	tr
⊤̿	dbl tr
Ⱥ	3 tr cluster
◊	pineapple
◊	popcorn
◉	picot with ss

CARE OF CROCHET

Removal of stains

It is important before washing the crochet lace that any stains are removed and a few practical hints are listed below.

Tea or coffee stains

Remove immediately by washing in soapy, tepid water. Rinse thoroughly.

Ink stains

Soak the stain in a cup of warm milk, leaving it for some time. Add lemon juice in which a little salt has been added. Rinse frequently.

Wine and fruit stains

First cover the stain with salt, then rub with a piece of damp soap. Leave for a few hours and afterwards wash with a bleaching solution.

Rust marks

Damp the mark with hot water, cover with a pinch of powdered wood sorrel (from the chemist) and leave for some minutes. Rinse well in running water. Take care to keep the powder away from children. It is very poisonous.

Ballpoint ink

Act quickly or the stain may be impossible to remove. Most types respond to dabbing with methylated spirits applied on a cotton-wool bud.

Blood stains

Do not leave the mark to dry; sponge immediately with cold salt water, soak in warm water for a while and then launder in warm suds. A simple remedy is to moisten a pad of cotton-wool with saliva and keep pressing the mark until it disappears.

Simple washing

After removing the stains, wash cottons with hot soapy water, to which a few drops of ammonia have been added.

Wool is washed in warm water and articles only squeezed

Washing temperatures

100°C	boil
95°C	Very hot; water heated to near boiling temperatures
60°C	hot; hotter than the hand can bear
50°C	hand hot
40°C	warm
30°C	cool

Starching

Simple starching

Dissolve starch in cold water so that it becomes milky. Dip the wet or dry garment into this and squeeze well. Wrap in a clean cloth for an hour, and then press with a very hot iron.

Boiled starch

When a greater degree of stiffening is required, use boiled starch. Dissolve starch in cold water, mix well with a wooden spoon until free from lumps. Heat half of this amount, and bring to boil for a few minutes. Leave to cool, and pour it into the rest of the cold starch and add more cold water until a thick solution is obtained. Place the article into this, squeeze, wrap in clean cloth, and leave for an hour, then press.

Sugar solution

Take two tablespoons of granulated sugar and one of boiling water (do not use brown sugar). Pour the water over the sugar in a small pan, place over a low heat and stir until the sugar is dissolved. Do not let the sugar burn. Place the article in the sugar solution and make sure that every part is damp. Squeeze out gently.

The pressing of crochet

For cotton

Having folded the article in a damp cloth and left it for an hour, take it from the cloth and proceed to block it to shape. Working from the centre outwards, firmly smooth the article out to its original shape. All pattern should be carefully stretched out to the original measurement; if the edge is picoted, every picot must be painstakingly smoothed out and pinned to shape. This should then be placed on a soft pad, right side down, and non-rusting pins used to pin the shape to the pad. Crochet has an embossed surface so heavy pressing is not required, and it is usually sufficient to place the damp cloth on the article with the iron held just off the surface of the article. It is better then to leave it on the pad overnight to dry naturally.

For wool

Each section of a woollen garment is lightly pressed with a damp cloth and warm iron before joining. This makes for a more professional finish and helps when matching the seams for joining. It only remains then to press those seams and edgings, but crochet should still not be overpressed.

When exhibiting it is not possible to emphasise enough the need for careful pressing.

International textile care labelling code

Symbol	Washing temperature		Rinse	Fabric
1 / 95°	Machine very hot 95°C	Hand hand hot 50°C or boil	normal	for white cotton and linen
2 / 60°	hot 60°C	hand hot 50°C	normal	for linen, cotton
3 / 60°	hot 60°C	hand hot 50°C	cold to minimize creasing	for white nylon or Polyester/cotton
4 / 50°	hand hot 50°C	hand hot 50°C	cold to minimize creasing	coloured nylon, cotton/rayon mixture; acrylic/cotton mixture
5 / 40°	warm 40°C	warm 40°C	normal	cotton, linen to safeguard colours
6 / 40°	warm 40°C	warm 40°C	cold to minimize creasing	polyester/wool
7 / 40°	warm 40°C	warm 40°C	normal	for wool, wool/cotton, silk do not hand wring
8 / 30°	cool 30°C	cool 30°C	cold to minimize creasing	silk
9 / 95°	very hot 95°C	hand hot 50°C	cold to minimize creasing	cotton with special finish
(hand symbol)	Do not machine wash			
(crossed-out symbol)	Do not wash at all			

SUPPLIERS

In the case of being unable to obtain yarns and equipment, contact the following suppliers.

UK

Yarns, 2-ply Shetland wool, books

ANI
Art Needlework Industries Ltd,
7 St Michael's Mansions,
Ship Street,
Oxford, oX1 3DG.

Cottons, hooks, books

MACE AND NAIRN
89 Crane Street,
Salisbury,
Wilts, SP1 2PY.

Hairpin crochet frames, flower looms and Easi-weave frames

B AND M HANDICRAFTS,
235 Columbia Road,
Ensbury Park,
Bournemouth.

Tambour hooks, net

COOPERS,
82–84 High Street,
Witham,
Essex.

Wools, synthetic yarns, cotton. Mail order

BEST WOOLS,
26 Frenchgates,
Doncaster,
Yorks.

USA

Wool, synthetics, silk

ROBIN & RUSS HANDWEAVERS,
533 North Adams Street,
McMinnville,
Oregon 97128

Swedish wools

BERGA ULLMAN,
P.O. Box 918,
North Adams,
Massachusetts 01247

Hooks, books

LACIS,
2990 Adeline Street,
Berkeley,
California 94703.

Wools, mohair and synthetics

B & YARN CO.,
151 Essex Street,
New York,
New York 10002.

Novelty yarns and wools

CONTESSA YARNS,
P.O. Box 37,
Lebanon,
Connecticut 06249.

Wools, mohair

CLINTON WILKINSON,
6429 Virginia Avenue,
Charlotte,
North Carolina.

AUSTRALIA

WOOLCRAFT PTY LTD,
250 Elizabeth Street, Melbourne.

MYLADY'S KNITTING WOOL CENTRE,
238 Flinders Street, Melbourne.

KERSHAWS WOOL SHOPS,
447 Pacific Highway,
Crows Nest,
Sydney.

KNITTING NOOK,
17 Adelaide Arcade,
Adelaide.

THE ENGLISH WOOLSHOP,
Rowes Arcade,
235 Edward street,
Brisbane.

NEEDLEWOMAN SHOP,
Shop G17,
Wesley Centre, Perth.

GROUP INFORMATION

Information about lacemaking, including crochet classes and courses in the UK can be obtained from the Lace Guild, through the British Craft Centre, at 43 Earlham Street, London WC2H 9LD.

For information from the Lace Society (formerly the Lace Society of Wales) apply to the Chairman, Mrs Amy Straker, 51 Beechey Road, Wrexham, Clwyd, Wales.

For information on Crochet Crafts, apply to the Knitting and Crochet Guild, Secretary, Mrs Karen Hodgson, 6 Crooklands View, Clifton, Penrith, England, CA10 2QE.

Information about lacemaking, crochet and tatting in the USA can be obtained from the International Old Lacers, Mrs E Reichenbach, Director USA, 4620 – 130th, SE Bellvue, Washington 98006. The UK Director is Mrs. Jean Pegg, 90 Kimberly Road, Southbourne, Bournemouth, Dorset, UK.

Please enclose a stamped addressed envelope when sending for information.

BIBLIOGRAPHY

Anchor Manual of Needlework, Batsford, 1968.

Auld, Rhodda, *The History of Needlwork Tools*, David & Charles, Newton Abbott, 1969.

Bath, Churchill Virginia, *Lace*, Cassell, Collier Macmillan, 1974.

Butterick's *The Art of Crocheting*, London and New York, 1891.

Caulfield, S. & Saward, B., *Dictionary of Needlework*, 2nd ed., A. Cowan, 1882.

Collingwood, Peter, *The Technique of Sprang*, Faber & Faber, 1974.

de Dillmont, Thérèse, *Encyclopaedia of Needlework*, D.M.C., 1891.

Dudding, Jean, *Creating Coggeshall Lace*, 1979.

Earnshaw, Pat, *The Identification of Lace*, Shire Publications, Princes Risborough, 1980.

Jackson, F. Nevill, *A History of Hand-made Lace*, L. Upcott Gill, 1900.

Kloster, Jane & Murray, Margaret, *New Crochet & Hairpin work*, John Calder, London, 1955.

Mellen, Lisa, *Knotting and Netting*, Van Nostrand Reinhold, 1972.

Palliser, Mrs E. Bury, *The History of Lace*, Samson Lowe, London, 1901.

Stearns, Ann, *The Batsford Book of Crochet*, Batsford, 1981.

Vinciolo, Frederico, *Renaissance Patterns for Lace and Embroidery, 1587*, facsimile reproduction, Dover Publications, 1971.

Wardle, Patricia, *Victorian Lace*, Herbert Jenkins, 1968.

Weldens, *Encyclopaedia of Needlework*, Waverly, 1942.

The Young Ladies Guide to the Worktable, 1885.

The Young Ladies Journal.

INDEX